# BOOK CLUB REBOOT

ALA Editions purchases fund advocacy, awareness, and accreditation programs for library professionals worldwide.

# BOOK CLUB Reboot

## 71 CREATIVE TWISTS

SARAH OSTMAN | STEPHANIE SABA

ALA Editions
CHICAGO 2019

**SARAH OSTMAN** is the communications manager in the American Library Association's Public Programs Office, where she serves as editor of ProgrammingLibrarian.org, a web resource for library professionals. Before joining the ALA and the library field in 2014, she spent nearly a decade as a newspaper reporter, editor, and freelance writer. Ostman has an MA in journalism from Columbia College in Chicago and a BA in sociology and theater from Smith College in Massachusetts.

**STEPHANIE SABA** is a community program supervisor at San Mateo County Libraries in California. Over the last fifteen years, she has led book clubs in three different communities, including two twenty- to thirty-something book clubs, a mother-daughter book club, an adult book club, and a senior book club. She has served on the ALSC's Early Childhood Programs and Services Committee, the CLA's California Young Reader Medal Committee, the ALSC's Public Awareness Committee, and the ALA's Public and Cultural Programs Advisory Committee. Saba has an MLIS degree from San Jose State University and a BA in English literature from San Francisco State University.

© 2019 by the American Library Association

Extensive effort has gone into ensuring the reliability of the information in this book; however, the publisher makes no warranty, express or implied, with respect to the material contained herein.

ISBNs
978-0-8389-1856-2 (paper)
978-0-8389-1887-6 (PDF)
978-0-8389-1886-9 (ePub)
978-0-8389-1888-3 (Kindle)

**Library of Congress Cataloging-in-Publication Data**

Names: Ostman, Sarah, author. | Saba, Stephanie, author.
Title: Book club reboot : 71 creative twists / Sarah Ostman and Stephanie Saba.
Description: Chicago : ALA Editions, 2019. | Includes bibliographical references and index.
Identifiers: LCCN 2018059751 | ISBN 9780838918562 (print : alk. paper) | ISBN 9780838918869
    (epub) | ISBN 9780838918876 (pdf) | ISBN 9780838918883 (kindle)
Subjects: LCSH: Libraries—Activity programs—United States—Case studies. | Book clubs (Discussion
    groups—United States—Case studies. | Libraries and community—United States—Case studies.
Classification: LCC Z716.33 .O85 2019 | DDC 025.5--dc23
LC record available at https://lccn.loc.gov/2018059751

Book design by Alejandra Diaz in the Chaparral Pro and Gotham typefaces.

♾ This paper meets the requirements of ANSI/NISO Z39.48-1992 (Permanence of Paper).

Printed in the United States of America
23  22  21  20  19      5  4  3  2  1

For my mom, who is responsible for my love of books and libraries,
and my husband, who participated in my first book club
when I was worried no one would attend the meetings.
ﻋ **S.S.** ﻉ


For my mom, and Eric, and all the kind, brilliant librarians
who made this book so fun to write.
ﻋ **S.O.** ﻉ

# CONTENTS

---

CHAPTER 8

## ENCOURAGE ACTIVISM | 61

CHAPTER 9

## MEET THEM WHERE THEY ARE | 71

CHAPTER 10

## SHORT ON TIME | 79

CHAPTER 11

## PUT IT ONLINE | 85

CHAPTER 12

## GET THEM MEETING AT AN EARLY AGE | 91

# PREFACE

**We wish it** were possible to capture every wonderful, out-of-the-box book club idea in a single collection; alas, it is not. Instead, we have done our best to gather a wide cross-section of ideas to inspire you to rethink your book club offerings and come up with new directions to better meet your library's and community's needs.

We began compiling this collection in early 2018 by putting out a call to the library field. Drawing on social media, electronic mailing lists, e-newsletters, and websites, we invited library professionals and others to complete an online survey telling us about the creative book clubs they were hosting. We were floored by the number of responses we received—nearly 250 book clubs from across the United States. We supplemented this list through our own research, reaching out to the creators of unique book groups that we heard about through colleagues or found online.

From there we began the arduous process of deciding which book clubs to include. As you might imagine, many of the book clubs we considered were unique in similar ways—meeting in similar locales, reaching out to the same audiences, and so on. While we have done our best to compile a diverse group, we regret that we couldn't include more of the book clubs that, we learned, are hosting readers across the country. If you know of a unique book club that we missed, please tell us about it at publicprograms@ala.org.

And to the dozens of librarians, library workers, volunteers, bookstore staff, and other book club aficionados who helped make this project such a joy to work on—thank you.

**—SARAH OSTMAN AND STEPHANIE SABA**

# ACKNOWLEDGMENTS

**Thank you to** the following people, whose smarts, creativity, and willingness to share made this book possible.

**Audrey Barbakoff,** King County (Wash.) Library System

**Jeanne Besaw,** Crystal Bridges Museum of American Art Library, Bentonville, Ark.

**Lorene Broersma,** Upland (Calif.) Public Library

**Cleo Brooks,** Seattle (Wash.) Public Library

**Pam Brooks,** Scotch Plains (N.J.) Public Library

**Anna Brown,** Katy Budget Books, Houston, Texas

**Julene Brown,** Skagway (Alaska) Public Library

**Tyler Brown,** Albany County (Wyo.) Public Library

**Anne Canada,** Paris (Ark.) Middle School Library

**Lisa Carr,** Seymour Public Library District, Auburn, N.Y.

**Caroline Chatterton,** Stewart B. Lang Memorial Library, Cato, N.Y.

**Megan Coleman,** Howe Library, Hanover, N.H.

**James Allen Davis,** Denver (Colo.) Public Library

**Robyn DeCourcy,** Autism Society of Minnesota, St. Paul, Minn.

**Katie DeVriese,** Alamance County (N.C.) Public Libraries, May Memorial Branch

**Natalie Draper,** Richmond (Va.) Public Library

**Jina DuVernay,** Levi Watkins Learning Center at Alabama State University, Montgomery, Ala.

**Hadiya Evans,** Denver (Colo.) Public Library

**Thomas Fish,** Next Chapter Book Club, Westerville, Ohio

**Courtney Fitzgerald,** Bentonville (Ark.) Public Library

**Suzanne Flynn,** Huntsville-Madison County (Ala.) Public Library

**Eileen Fontenot,** Thomas Crane Public Library, Quincy, Mass.

**Kristen Gerlinger,** Leander (Tex.) Public Library

**Don Giacomini,** Gwinnett County (Ga.) Public Library

**Jack Granath,** Bonner Springs (Kan.) City Library

**Renee Grassi,** Dakota County (Minn.) Library

**Gwin Grimes,** Jeff Davis County Library, Fort Davis, Tex.

**Gizelle Guyette,** Morristown Centennial Library, Morrisville, Vt.

**Alyson Hamlin,** Calimesa Library, Riverside County (Calif.) Library System

**Arianne Hartsell-Gundy,** Duke University Libraries, Durham, N.C.

**Dorri Hegyi,** Dayton (Ohio) Metro Library

**Jackie Hemond,** Kent Memorial Library, Suffield, Conn.

**Shanika Heyward,** Indianapolis (Ind.) Public Library

**Andrea Hirsh,** Juneau (Alaska) Public Library

**Kyle Homewood,** Arizona Opera, Phoenix, Ariz.

**Nancy Howe,** Baldwinsville (N.Y.) Public Library

**Nan Jackson,** Starr Library, Rhinebeck, N.Y.

**Brian Johnson,** Lakeside Junior High School, Springdale, Ark.

**Jeff Kamin,** Books & Bars, Saint Paul and Minneapolis, Minn.

**Melissa Kammerer,** Alamance County (N.C.) Public Library

**Katie Karkheck,** Valley Cottage (N.Y.) Library

**Lisa Kobrin,** Alamance County (N.C.) Public Library

**Matthew LaBrake,** Berkeley College Library, Paramus, N.J.

**Leah LaFera,** Schenectady County (N.Y.) Public Library

**Geoff Larson,** Bushwick Book Club, Seattle, Wash.

**Cindy Linker,** Hackett (Ark.) High School Library

**Ashley Maraffino,** Valley Cottage (N.Y.) Library

**Shelly Mathis,** Grand County (Colo.) Library District

**Joyce McCombs,** Delta Community Library, Delta Junction, Alaska

**Genna Mickey,** Sugar Grove (Ill.) Public Library

**Shannon Ng,** Idyllwild Library, Riverside County (Calif.) Library System

**Brittany Patrick,** Wells Branch Community Library, Austin, Tex.

**Emily Pedersen,** Grand County (Colo.) Library District

**Caryl-Rose Pofcher,** Jones Library, Amherst, Mass.

**Macy Purtle,** North Little Rock (Ark.) High School Library

**Diane Ranney,** Jonathan Bourne Public Library, Bourne, Mass.

**Andrew Richmond,** Rye (N.H.) Public Library

**Tracy Robinson,** Elizabeth (N.J.) Public Library

**Cathleen Russ,** Troy (Mich.) Public Library

**Meaghan Schwelm,** Boston (Mass.) Public Library, Adams Street Branch

**Kirsten Seidel,** Cabot (Ark.) Public Library

**Marissa Skinner,** Capital Region Board of Cooperative Educational Services, Albany, N.Y.

**Maureen Socha,** Orange County (N.C.) Public Library

**Sue Staehly,** Brainerd Memorial Library, Haddam, Conn.

**Konrad Stump,** Springfield-Greene County (Mo.) Library

**Nancy Tabb,** Johnson County (Wyo.) Library

**Colleen Tell,** Idyllwild Library, Riverside County (Calif.) Library System

**Monica Tolva,** Vernon Hills (Ill.) High School Library Media Center

**Sara Truog,** Milton (Mass.) Public Library

**Jace Turner,** Santa Barbara (Calif.) Public Library

**Hilary Umbreit,** Sharon (Mass.) Public Library

**Nancy Venable,** Campbell County (Wyo.) Public Library

**Brendle Wells,** Sacramento (Calif.) Public Library, Robbie Waters Pocket-Greenhaven Library

**Jenifer Whitmore,** Oasis Coalition of Boston (Mass.)

**Judy Wile,** Camas (Wash.) Public Library

**Rachel Wolgemuth,** Laurel Hill and West Laurel Hill Cemeteries, Philadelphia and Bala Cynwyd, Pa.

**Marika Zemke,** Commerce Township (Mich.) Community Library

# INTRODUCTION

**It's a story** many librarians know all too well.

For years, the Seymour Public Library District in Auburn, New York, had a book club, and it was good. Members would gather at the library on Monday evenings to discuss adult fiction and bestsellers like *The Kite Runner* and *Beloved*. Sometimes they liked the books, sometimes they hated the books, but the discussion flourished, and the friendships grew.

Then, after nearly a decade of blissful book-clubbing, everything changed.

"Life happened," recalls library director Lisa Carr. "A longtime member becomes the treasurer of something at the high school and can't come on Mondays. Someone else joined a choir. Suddenly attendance was a problem."

The library moved the book club to Wednesday nights, and they tried meeting at a different time. Nothing worked. The club dwindled to just a handful of regular attendees, and the conversations lacked the enthusiasm they once had. Then, for two consecutive months, just a single person showed up.

That's when Carr realized they needed to make a change. She needed something different than the typical book club—a new theme, location, or twist that would jolt readers in her community out of their rut and reinspire a love of collective reading. She needed a book club reboot.

## BOOK CLUBS ON THE RISE

While the Seymour Public Library District's book club was faltering, some others across the country were flourishing—at least according to the statistics.

In 2014, the *New York Times* estimated that a whopping 5 million Americans were members of a book club, though that number is hard to confirm. Other studies have delivered more quantifiable evidence of book clubs' rise in popularity. According to an ongoing survey by the online magazine BookBrowse.com, which has been tracking book club activity for more than a decade, participation in U.S. book clubs by regular readers—defined as people who read one or more books per month—rose steadily between 2004 and 2009, from 33 to 55 percent; since then, participation has reached a plateau, inching up just slightly to 57 percent in 2015. About one-third of book club members reported belonging to two or more clubs.

But you don't have to look at statistics to see that book clubs have gone mainstream. Their surge in popularity is no doubt fueled by many factors: book-loving celebrity trendsetters like Oprah Winfrey who, beginning in the late 1990s, inspired the reading habits of hordes of fans; the ease of online book clubs that let people indulge in shared experiences without leaving their homes; and a growing embrace of nerdiness in youth and popular culture. In recent years, reading groups have sprouted up by the thousands on Twitter, Facebook, and of course, Goodreads; they have intersected with the news in "Now Read This," a joint offering of the *PBS NewsHour* and the *New York Times*; and they have found a spotlight through *The Great American Read*, a televised series—with a corresponding Facebook book club—that called on Americans to vote for their own top novel. Book clubs even served as the inspiration for a 2018 film, *Book Club*, with a star-studded cast including Jane Fonda and Diane Keaton.

With so many options available, it can be difficult to find your niche in the book club world. Molly Lundquist, the creator of LitLovers.com, an online resource for book clubs that has profiled hundreds of mostly private clubs, says that the most successful clubs manage to balance two competing interests: fostering social connections through meaningful book discussions, and offering some good, old-fashioned diversion. "People have been hungry for community, and books give that to people," Lundquist says. "Then sometimes you get tired of substantial conversation, and you just want to have fun."

## WHY CHANGE UP YOUR BOOK CLUB?

First, let's be clear: there's absolutely nothing wrong with a "traditional" book club. Book clubs serve many purposes: to get people reading, to create a space for individuals to share ideas, to provide an opportunity to socialize, and to build connections between the host organization and its community. As long as your club is serving at least one of these goals, then hosting your run-of-the-mill book group is more than fine—it's fantastic.

That said, there are many reasons why you might want to make a change.

### People Aren't Coming

It can sting a bit, but often your book club members make the decision for you that it's time to pull the plug—by not showing up. Facilitating a book talk is hard work, and it's even harder when you have to carry a ninety-minute conversation by yourself. When Lisa Carr's attendance dropped down to three people, and finally to just one, it was hard to deny that the club needed to change. "It's hard to have a good discussion with so few people," Carr says. "We missed hearing more points of view. There was also less openness—I think we worried more about hurting one another's feelings."

The librarian Sherrie Langston Hardin faced a similar problem when attendance dwindled at her mystery book group at the San Antonio (Texas) Public Library. "Turnout is always unpredictable. I've had as many as 25 and as few as 2 or 3," says Hardin, who retired in 2018. "A dozen people voicing varying opinions on a topic provides for a livelier—and more interesting—group than three people who agree and just echo each other's thoughts."

This begs the perennial question: how small is too small? The exact make-or-break number will vary depending on your community, physical space, overall library programming attendance, and your book club's target audience. But as a general rule, it's challenging to host a book club with fewer than three regular attendees. Marika Zemke, adult services manager at the Commerce Township (Mich.) Community Library, decided to reinvent her Pre-Pub Book Club, a club that perused advance reader copies before they were published, when attendance dropped to that number.

"Three members were still showing up, but three isn't enough," Zemke recalls. "You have to consider how much work you're putting in for that number of people, especially when you could be spending your time on other programs." Zemke ended up combining the Pre-Pub Book Club with an existing daytime book club to accommodate more members' schedules. Today, the group has grown to eighteen members, and she is considering breaking it up into multiple clubs. (Read more about the Pre-Pub Book Club at book club no. 44 in this book.)

We should note that unpredictable attendance raises its own set of problems: how many books do you order when you have twelve attendees one month and two the next? If your book club hasn't fostered a core group of regulars, it might be time to consider a more engaging approach.

## You're Burned Out, Too Busy, or Bored

"How much work could it possibly be to run a book club?" they say. "It's just sitting around, talking about books."

Tell that to a librarian who hosts two or three clubs a month. Because as we all know, preparing for a book club can take a tremendous amount of work, between reading the books, locating copies for your members, developing discussion questions, marketing the club, communicating with members, and preparing the meeting space. And that's even before all the creative twists and add-ons that we'll be talking about throughout this book, from guest speakers to field trips to art projects.

If your book clubs are consuming too much of your day or simply leaving you drained instead of reinvigorated, it's time to consider a change. If time is your issue, there are book club formats—believe it or not—that will allow you to maintain a happy group of book lovers and still get home in time to feed your pets. Alyson Hamlin, branch manager of the Calimesa Library in California, ran a mystery book club until two factors compelled her to make a change: decreased attendance and a lack of staff manpower needed to keep the club afloat. A switch to a different format, where members read any book they want, not only led to increased attendance, but it also resulted in a volunteer offering to lead the group. (Read more about the Open Book Club at book club no. 22.)

At the opposite extreme, you might opt for an idea that requires hours of extra research and preparation, but it's worth it, because running the club feeds your soul. The choice is yours.

## It's Not Meeting Your Community's Needs

Consider what is important in your community at this moment. Is your library addressing these issues through its programming, and by extension, its book clubs?

When staff at the Denver Public Library paused to listen to their patrons in 2015, they learned that many were distraught about the recent deaths of Trayvon Martin, Michael Brown, and Sandra Bland. "We thought, we have to be more relevant in our community," says the adult services librarian James Allen Davis. "The library has to be more than just a place where the community can come; it has to be part of the community." In response, Davis and his colleagues created R.A.D.A. (Read. Awareness. Dialogue. Action.), a book discussion series that travels the city discussing issues and books of relevance to communities. (Read more about R.A.D.A. at book club no. 45.)

Jeanne Besaw, the head of library services at the Crystal Bridges Museum of American Art in Bentonville, Arkansas, realized that her library's "typical bestseller" book club was not helping to connect the largely low-income, white residents of Bentonville to the often boundary-pushing art exhibits at the museum.

"What if our focus was to help inform our public, as well as our staff and volunteers, about what's coming next at the museum?" she asked herself. Membership in the resulting IDEA (Inclusion, Diversity, Equity, and Accessibility) Book Club increased from 4 people to 22—surprising everyone, including Besaw. "I really expected it to fail, to be honest. I had no expectations at all." (Read more about the IDEA Book Club at book club no. 46.)

Often, it takes an eye-opening experience to become aware of a need. When Sue Staehly was diagnosed with breast cancer in 2010, she coped by surrounding herself with people going through similar circumstances, and she used her research skills to share health-related information with them. That experience led her to start the Healthy Exchange Book Club at the Brainerd Memorial Library in Haddam, Connecticut. The group's members engage in healthy activities together and read health-related books, sometimes about illnesses, such as Alzheimer's or Parkinson's, that are affecting members or their loved ones. "These are the topics that our members are struggling with, so we provide an opportunity to learn about it together," Staehly says. Having come to understand firsthand the need for support, Staehly was able to offer it at her library. (Read more about the Healthy Exchange Book Club at book club no. 28.)

## Your Meeting Time or Location Aren't Working Out

Take an objective look at the book clubs you offer. Do they conflict with certain basic realities of your community? If so, you may need to make some adjustments.

For example, if you work in a devoutly Christian locality, a Sunday afternoon book club is probably destined to fail because most people will be having post-church family time. If your target audience uses public transit, you likely won't have much luck hosting a book club at a remote library branch that is only reachable by car. And if you're hosting an after-school club for teens in a community with gang violence, don't overlook gang territory lines, and certainly don't expect kids to cross them after dark.

Even with the most careful planning, logistical issues may pop up that force us to adjust on a moment's notice. When the Kent Memorial Library in Suffield, Connecticut, was relocated to a temporary building for a renovation, library director Jackie Hemond had little choice but to think outside the box. She ended up partnering with a local historic house museum to create Books in the Parlor, a book club that reads historic books in the parlor of a landmark eighteenth-century home. "I thought, 'This is perfect. We can collaborate with the Phelps-Hatheway

House to keep us alive,'" Hemond says. (Read more about Books in the Parlor at book club no. 3.)

The bottom line is that issues like these are bound to affect us all, at one time or another. We can let them get the best of us, or we can use them to innovate.

## CHOOSING THE RIGHT BOOK CLUB FOR YOUR COMMUNITY

So, you've decided it's time to make some changes. What now? Here are some considerations that might be useful as you prepare for your new endeavor.

### Poll Your Current and Former Members and Tie Up Loose Ends

Before you make any firm plans, we suggest talking to your current and former book club members. As proven book club enthusiasts, they are your best resource for ideas about what a successful next venture would look like. This will also give you the opportunity, if you haven't done so already, to gently mention to current attendees that the library may cancel or change the existing club.

If you know your book club's members fairly well, a personal e-mail, phone call, or in-person chat is warranted; if not, you could create a simple online survey to solicit feedback from your mailing list. You'll want to know what drew them to the book club originally, what they like about it, and what they'd like to change. If they stopped attending, ask if they're comfortable sharing why. You can also ask specific questions to feel out their reactions to some new ideas you're considering. Let them know that you're asking because you want to better understand what book lovers in your community want, so you can offer stronger book clubs in the future.

You may only get a handful of responses; that's okay. Most importantly, be honest, and be open to whatever you hear. You may find that you're reading best-sellers when some readers really like romance; or that you're *reading* books when they'd rather be listening to them; or that they'd really prefer to be discussing the latest Dean Koontz book with a nice merlot, or a pilsner, or a crepe. Make a list of everything you've heard and be sure to say thank you.

## OUT WITH THE OLD

Here's a sample e-mail you could send to your book club members upon winding down a current group:

Hi Mary,

I hope all is well with you! I'm reaching out with a few questions about your experience with the Plainville Public Library's Women's Book Club.

Our attendance has been a bit low lately, so I'm looking at different ways to restructure our club going forward. Your answers would really help me get a better handle on what our readers are looking for, so please be candid!

1. What originally drew you to the Women's Book Club?

2. What do you enjoy about the book club?

3. What would you like to change about it (e.g., different book selections, different meeting day or time, meet in a different location, etc.)?

4. Would you be interested in attending a book club that meets at The Vineyard wine bar?

5. What day/time is most convenient for you?

Any and all feedback is appreciated. If possible, please send me your feedback by Friday, January 11. Thank you, and I hope to run into you at the library soon.

Best,
Gina

## Put on Your Thinking Cap

Now is the time, as Winnie the Pooh says, to "think, think, think." Grab a notebook and pen—or a coworker and a pot of coffee—and start brainstorming. Your goal should be to develop three or four solid ideas that are logistically feasible for your library, that are effective in terms of reaching a desired audience, and that get you personally excited.

Here are some questions to get you started:

- **Audience.** What community groups are already meeting in your community? Is there a particular social group, subculture, or fan fiction group that could benefit from a book club? Where are the holes in your library's current programming? Are you overlooking teens, twenty- and thirty-somethings, or older adults? Do you have enough programming that appeals to men? What about patrons with special needs?
- **Community assets.** Does your community have any unique aspects that you could draw on? Is there a unique meeting space that people are eager to see? A new restaurant or bar that would add a fun element to your gathering? A historical connection or community event that you could tap?
- **Culture.** What do members of your community enjoy doing? Where do they spend their time?
- **Partners.** Does your library have existing partnerships that you could tap for a book club? Are there organizations you have been looking for an excuse to approach? Consider the usual suspects—local nonprofits, higher education, parks and recreation, schools—as well as businesses, social service organizations, and your region's largest employers.
- **Genres and book titles.** What are your patrons most interested in reading? Which genres in your library's collection get the most traction? Are there any topics or genres that would be an automatic flop in your community?
- **Staffing.** What level of staff commitment can your library offer? Do you need a book club that minimizes prep time? Do you need a volunteer to facilitate the group?
- **Funding.** What level of funding is your library able to provide? Do you need to find grant funding or a partner organization to cover related costs?
- **Strategic plan.** How should this book club tie into your library's strategic plan? Do you need approval from your library director, board, or Friends group? How should you involve them in this change process?

Answering these questions should help you narrow your focus and decide on your next book club venture; if that's the case, your final hurdle will likely be gaining buy-in from your supervisors.

Or if the opposite happens, and you're more overwhelmed than ever when it comes to making a choice, take a cue from libraries that have walked this path before you.

## YOU DON'T HAVE TO REINVENT THE WHEEL

Chances are, you've heard of the trend of hosting book clubs in bars and breweries. Libraries all across the country are doing it, using clever names like Books on Tap and Books & Brews. In fact, we profile a couple such clubs in this book. Why are so many libraries moving their book clubs to these booze-filled establishments? Because it works!

Our point is, you are under no obligation to come up with a truly original book club idea. Popular ideas become popular for a reason, after all. If you're looking for a tried-and-true book club model, look no further than the following ideas. They might not win you points for originality, but they're a (proven) good time.

- **Book club in a bar.** Get on the bandwagon and relocate your meetings to a local watering hole. Look for spots with a manageable noise level, or ask the management if they have a quiet spot or private room you can reserve. Be open to creative twists and tie-ins. If you have a particularly enthusiastic brewery partner, for example, they may be willing to recommend a beer to match your month's reading. A word of caution: watch your own consumption. "I limit myself to one—one, then done," says Leah LaFera, who runs the Read 'n' Greet Book Club at the Schenectady County (N.Y.) Public Library.
- **Cookbook club.** A twist on a genre-specific book club, cookbook clubs are a way to engage not just readers, but home chefs and foodies. There are plenty of possible variations depending on your library's facilities and rules. Invite people to cook a recipe from a single cookbook each month, or compare recipes from different cookbooks within a certain cuisine. Members can bring the recipe to share, potluck-style, or if you have a kitchen, you might invite a local chef to do a demonstration.
- **Clubs without required reading.** Also known as "reading circles," these clubs forgo the experience of shared reading and discussion, and instead give readers the chance to share whatever it is they are currently reading. This option enables members to build their reading lists with tips from others, and it also gives club hosts a break from most of the prep work we typically associate with book clubs, such as locating copies of the book and writing discussion questions.
- **Book-to-movie club.** We know, the movie is never quite as good. But comparing a book to its film adaptation can spark lively conversation and be a draw for your community's film buffs. You can screen the films at your library or partner with a local theater, which may be willing to offer reduced-rate

tickets for a screening during off-hours. If you screen the film yourself, remember to get the appropriate screening permissions.

- **Celebrity book clubs.** Hey, if Oprah, Sarah Jessica Parker, and Mindy Kaling want to make our jobs easier, who are we to stop them? Celebrities may not facilitate your book club meetings, but their reading picks, shared through their established book clubs or informally on social media, can provide a go-to reading list and give your club a little name recognition to boot.

## ONE LIBRARY'S SOLUTION

Whatever happened to the book club at the Seymour Public Library District in Auburn, New York—the Monday evening group whose attendance had dropped to just one person before library director Lisa Carr decided to shake things up?

The library decided to recast the struggling club to support the goals of another library program, a year-round reading challenge called Read More! Patrons are invited to read twenty-six books throughout the year that fit into different reading categories. The affiliated Read More! Book Club meets on Wednesday evenings to help readers stay on track to complete the challenge. The library also moved the gatherings to a local brewpub to add some appeal. (Read more about this at book club no. 26.)

That was one library's answer to their book club woes. What will your solution be? Before you decide, let's look at a host of other unique approaches for creating a book club that your community will love. The chapters in this book examine seventy-one different book clubs, all of them sequentially numbered. We explore the book clubs' origins and goals, their formats, and some favorite book titles they have read together. We also share insights from the clubs' hosts about what they have learned along the way—because as you will see, a great book club is often a work in progress.

# CHAPTER ONE

# CHANGE OF SCENERY

**S**ure, your library's community room is a perfectly adequate space for your book club. We're book lovers—all we need is a quiet room and some decent lighting, right?

Perhaps. But if your book club location is feeling a bit stale, consider relocating it outside your library walls. As countless libraries have already discovered, your neighborhood pub is certainly one option (if you can find one with a low enough noise level). Other ideas, as you'll see in this chapter, are even further outside the box: historic houses, serene wildlife sanctuaries, kitschy doughnut shops, and more.

# Read 'n' Greet Book Club

**SCHENECTADY COUNTY PUBLIC LIBRARY | SCHENECTADY, NEW YORK**

**COMMUNITY TYPE: URBAN**

With a popular off-Broadway theater, hopping nightlife, and a flourishing dining scene, downtown Schenectady is enjoying a bit of a renaissance. The local library has leveraged this buzz with Read 'n' Greet, a book club that hops around to new restaurants, appealing to both book lovers and foodies who want to sample their city's latest eateries.

Visiting new restaurants is a gamble, says librarian Leah LaFera—what if the space is too loud or the waitstaff is rude?—but it's worth it to keep the club fresh. And it seems to be working; Read 'n' Greet's monthly meetings frequently max out their registration cap of fourteen attendees.

To determine whether a new restaurant may be a good book club host, LaFera first visits the restaurant as a customer. If it seems like a fit for her group—laid-back atmosphere, good beer list—she talks to the restaurant staff about her other requirements. "We need a private or semiprivate room where we can set up the tables in a square, ideally, rather than a long rectangle," LaFera says. "We also need to have the restaurant's music turned down in our room so we can hear each other, and we need separate checks." She holds Read 'n' Greet meetings on Tuesday evenings, which is typically a slow night for restaurants.

At first, LaFera tried spelling out her needs in a note to the restaurant's manager, but she quickly learned that this wasn't effective. "Restaurant managers often won't read your e-mails," she says. "Go in person. It helps foster that personal connection." To help build a good relationship, LaFera encourages book club members to tip their waitstaff well, and she often brings along extra advance reader copies to give to restaurant staff.

The most important thing LaFera has learned is to go with the flow. "In the beginning we were really organized and tried to control the environment we were meeting in, only to show up and learn the restaurant didn't have enough waitstaff or they had set up the tables wrong," she says. "We got flexible real fast. It isn't like holding a program inside your library where you can control everything from the table setup to the temperature."

Recently, a couple of new restaurants have even reached out to the library to offer themselves as a host. "It's nice that we're developing these relationships,"

LaFera says. "Now I have these contacts that I can approach to bring bigger programs out into the community."

## Tales & Trails Book Club

**SUGAR GROVE PUBLIC LIBRARY | SUGAR GROVE, ILLINOIS**
**COMMUNITY TYPE: RURAL AND SUBURBAN**

If you feel like your book club is missing something, take note: a little fresh air and exercise can do wonders for the soul. Add dogs and babies into the mix, and you're sure to have a smiling group of readers.

Located in a small town of 9,000 about 50 miles west of Chicago, the Sugar Grove Public Library has the good fortune of being located near the Virgil L. Gilman Trail, an eleven-mile nature trail that winds through wetlands and patches of native prairie. On Wednesday mornings, once a month between April and October, members of the Tales & Trails Book Club meet at a trailhead for a sixty-minute walk along the trail, where they can often spot cranes, swans, and other wildlife. Dogs and strollers are welcome, and the library provides trail mix and bottled water.

While they walk, members chat about the month's read—which has been selected from a wide range of genres in order to encourage readers to "go off the beaten path," says Genna Mickey, the library's assistant director. Since the club meets during the workday, the original intention was to reach stay-at-home parents, but retirees and people with flexible work schedules are the group's core members. "Our target audience is people who enjoy both reading and being active," Mickey says. "Books can be such a sedentary activity while reading! All of my attendees have said they enjoy walking and being out on the path, and that is the draw for them." (In fact, if it rains, the group reschedules their walk instead of having a regular, seated discussion indoors.)

The logistics of walking and talking can prove a challenge, but Mickey says having a small group of readers makes it work. "It is pretty easy to walk and talk and still allow for the whole group to hear each other," she says. "Ultimately, if the club were larger, we would have to maybe pair off and alternate throughout the meeting so people had a chance to discuss with everyone."

It's fun to stop and say hello to other hikers (and their dogs) along the trail, Mickey says. These encounters also provide an opportunity to promote the club. "Take flyers with you and pass them out to people who you pass," she suggests.

## Books in the Parlor

**KENT MEMORIAL LIBRARY | SUFFIELD, CONNECTICUT**

**COMMUNITY TYPE: RURAL AND SUBURBAN**

When a construction project forced the Kent Memorial Library to a smaller, temporary location in 2014, the new library director, Jackie Hemond, started brainstorming creative ways to publicize the fact that the library was still there for the community. At the same time, Hemond was eager to offer new daytime programming that would appeal to older adults, instead of the children's programming and evening events the library typically offered.

And so Books in the Parlor—a book club partnership between the library and the Phelps-Hatheway House—was born. Located in the village center of Suffield, the Hatheway House is a historic house museum that was built by a wealthy Connecticut merchant in 1761. Today, the museum displays an extensive collection of antiques that illustrate the luxurious lifestyle lived by the original inhabitants.

The book club—currently a group of ten women—gathers in one of the Hatheway House's elegant rooms on Tuesday afternoons, when the museum is closed to the public. (When the museum closes for the winter months, the club rotates between members' own living rooms.) In keeping with their eighteenth-century surroundings, they read historical fiction and nonfiction that relate to the periods when the house was lived in. The group's favorites have included *Midnight Rising: John Brown and the Raid That Sparked the Civil War* by Tony Horwitz, about the abolitionist John Brown whose surprise strike on Harpers Ferry propelled the nation toward war; and *March* by Geraldine Brooks, a novel that reimagines *Little Women* from the perspective of Louisa May Alcott's father.

"Our members are keenly interested in American history, and their experience and knowledge add to the group's discussion," Hemond says. One member is an expert on historic quilts and has brought samples to add to their discussions; other members are history buffs who provide insight into the histories of Connecticut, Suffield, and the Hatheway House.

Since Books in the Parlor's members are all women, future book selections will focus on prominent women from New England history, including the Quaker abolitionist Prudence Crandall and the architect Theodate Pope Riddle. "It'll give us more of a feminist perspective," Hemond says.

## Nature Book Club

**STEWART B. LANG MEMORIAL LIBRARY | CATO, NEW YORK**

**COMMUNITY TYPE: RURAL**

When Caroline Chatterton started her job as director of the Lang Memorial Library in Cato, a small town 25 miles outside Syracuse, developing new library partnerships was a top priority. The children's programming coordinator, Gayle James, had an idea: why not pair up with the nearby Montezuma National Wildlife Refuge, a 10,000-acre wildlife preserve run by the U.S. Fish and Wildlife Service, where James worked part-time in the visitors' center?

The result was the Nature Book Club. The group—open to adults and young adults, and promoted to patrons of both the library and the refuge—started meeting quarterly in early 2018. The book selections focus on nature and environmental issues, and the meetings involve both a book discussion and an opportunity to get outside. "We're able to have meaningful discourse about a topic and then go out into the wildlife refuge and experience, firsthand, many of the themes, issues, and elements of our book discussions," Chatterton says.

Book titles are selected jointly by library and wildlife refuge staff, which allows for the partners to align their programming. For example, when the club read *Refuge: An Unnatural History of Family and Place*, a book-length essay by Terry Tempest Williams that covers themes of nature, death, and spirituality, refuge staff started the meeting with a serene drive through the preserve's Wildlife Drive. "It was so beautiful and peaceful," Chatterton says. "It put us in a great frame of mind before the discussion." At a later meeting, when book club members had been tasked with reading their choice of books about trees, refuge staff took members on a tree-focused tour.

Of course, all this collaboration requires work. "Because this book club is facilitated by two different organizations, it takes even more conversation, coordination, and planning," Chatterton says. "Always be vigilant about keeping the lines of communication open."

The Nature Book Club is still new, but Chatterton says it's shaping up to be the beginning of a strong partnership. "We're happy to say that we're reading, exploring, learning, and making connections thanks to this book club," she says. The library recently installed a Little Free Library at the wildlife refuge; down the line, Chatterton hopes the two organizations can offer more joint programming.

## Fine Liquorature Book Club

**THOMAS CRANE PUBLIC LIBRARY | QUINCY, MASSACHUSETTS**
**COMMUNITY TYPE: URBAN**

Eileen Fontenot describes the Fine Liquorature Book Club as "a youngish group that examines the complex world of literature and explores our bustling city." Since 2016, the group has served as a way for twenty- and thirty-somethings in this Boston suburb to meet, chat about literature, and forge friendships that go beyond books. "A lot of our attendees are newcomers to Quincy," says Fontenot, an adult services librarian. "They want to get to know their new community."

"Field trips" have provided a creative way to engage readers beyond the monthly Fine Liquorature meetings. When the group read *Citizen: An American Lyric*, they traveled to Emerson College in Boston to attend an event with author Claudia Rankine. "I knew this would be a popular event with the group because these young professionals are diverse and, for the most part, interested in progressive issues," Fontenot says. "One of our participants commented that he understood the book and the author's viewpoints much better after seeing her in person."

After reading Shakespeare's *Romeo and Juliet*, a member suggested they make it a summertime tradition to read Shakespeare and then see an annual free performance by the Commonwealth Shakespeare Company. "Now we do Shakespeare every summer," Fontenot says. "It enriches their experience with literature, and it's an extra way to hang out and have fun." As their next trip, the group plans to read Nathaniel Hawthorne's novel *The House of the Seven Gables* and then carpool to Salem, Massachusetts, to see the house that inspired it.

For their regular book discussions, the club meets at a local restaurant—one that's not too packed with sports fans, since their Monday evening gatherings overlap with football games for part of the year. The establishments have ranged from a local Chinese restaurant to a low-key sports bar. "We want them to eat and drink and feel more relaxed, and be loud if they want," Fontenot says, "in a place where no one's going to shush them."

## Outdoor Explorer Book Club

**ORANGE COUNTY PUBLIC LIBRARY | HILLSBOROUGH, NORTH CAROLINA**

**COMMUNITY TYPE: MIX OF URBAN AND RURAL**

Orange County, North Carolina, is home to a population of more than 130,000, including the cities of Durham and Chapel Hill and the University of North Carolina (UNC) at Chapel Hill. It's also home to numerous parks and trails that foster a significant community of hikers and nature lovers.

To engage this population, the Orange County Public Library created the Outdoor Explorer Book Club, a group for people who love reading and outdoor adventure. The book club discusses books related to the outdoors—generally nonfiction titles about hiking, survival, or nature—and incorporates an outdoor experience like a hike or walk.

In a community that is "a mix of artists, outdoor enthusiasts, retirees, and educated citizens," the Outdoor Explorer Book Club brings attendees together in a different venue each month, says adult and teen services librarian Maureen Socha. Locations have included Coker Arboretum on the UNC campus, the 152-acre Blackwood Farm Park, and the North Carolina Botanic Garden. Favorite book titles have included *Grandma Gatewood's Walk: The Inspiring Story of the Woman Who Saved the Appalachian Trail* by Ben Montgomery and *Jaguars Ripped My Flesh* by Tim Cahill.

Fun add-ons keep the group's meetings interesting. Group members rotate leading the discussion and add their own flair; when the group read *Lost in the Wild: Danger and Survival in the North Woods* by Cary J. Griffith, the discussion leader asked everyone to bring a survival item to the meeting. And the library sometimes hosts speakers to complement its book club readings; after the Outdoor Explorers read *The Beekeeper's Lament: How One Man and Half a Billion Honey Bees Help Feed America* by Hannah Nordhaus, the Orange County Beekeeper's Association came to the library to present a program called All About Bees.

# FIND A PARTNER

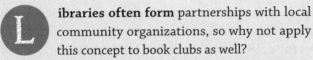

**L**ibraries often form partnerships with local community organizations, so why not apply this concept to book clubs as well?

While book clubs are a natural fit for libraries, whose staff can easily provide the knowledge of books along with the physical reading materials, it can be harder for other organizations to get a book club off the ground. On the other hand, libraries often struggle to find participants for their book clubs, while other local groups already have a built-in membership.

Finding a community partner for your book club is beneficial for everyone involved. Partnerships can enable the club to meet somewhere unique, have access to interesting guest speakers, and reach non-library users in the community.

# The Mayor's Book Club

**ALAMANCE COUNTY PUBLIC LIBRARIES | BURLINGTON, NORTH CAROLINA**
**COMMUNITY TYPE: URBAN**

When Mayor Ian Baltutis was elected, his office partnered with the local library to create a book club for his constituents. With the hope of inspiring members to engage in discussions on topics that affect their community such as economic development, social issues, and city planning, the mayor's office and library staff carefully select the books together each month. Melissa Kammerer, a programming librarian at the Alamance County Public Libraries, states: "The book club is now entering its third year and has partnered with many other local agencies to discuss a wide range of community issues, challenges and opportunities."

The book club is not afraid to confront controversial topics at their meetings. Because the mayor leads the discussions at the library or at The Blend, a local coffee shop, the meetings provide the community with a chance to share their opinions with their elected representative in a safe and comfortable space. The library also sometimes invites guest speakers with an expertise on particular topics to join their meetings and provide the club with background knowledge relevant to the month's book selection.

Over the years, the book discussions have led to amazing programs and connections. Melody Warnick's *This Is Where I Belong: Finding Home Wherever You Are* "inspired the program Belong in Burlington, a city-led partnership to welcome new residents and introduce them to various groups in the community," says Kammerer. A discussion of Peter Kageyama's *Love Where You Live: Creating Emotionally Engaging Places* "brought about the idea of Alamance County starting a local edition of The Awesome Fund, microgrants that residents can apply for in order to create unique community projects." The book club invited a local elementary school principal and one of his students, Jordan, to their discussion of Stephen Covey's *The Leader in Me: How Schools around the World Are Inspiring Greatness, One Child at a Time.* Jordan shared a presentation with the group that both highlighted his accomplishments at school and shared how the book had motivated him. Kammerer recalls, "By the time he was done, there wasn't a dry eye in the room!"

# The Agri-CULTURE Book Club

**BONNER SPRINGS CITY LIBRARY | BONNER SPRINGS, KANSAS**
**COMMUNITY TYPE: SUBURBAN**

One night, two librarians struck up a conversation with the director of the National Agricultural Center and Hall of Fame, which is located in Bonner Springs, Kansas. All three had gathered to attend an event at the Chamber of Commerce, but over the course of the evening, the idea for the Agri-CULTURE Book Club was also born. Several years later, the club's participants continue to gather every quarter at the National Agricultural Center and Hall of Fame to discuss books about farming and food.

During their first meeting in April 2016, the group discussed *The End of Plenty: The Race to Feed a Crowded World* by Joel K. Bourne. This book brought up topics that have continued to intrigue the group in subsequent meetings, including GMOs (genetically modified organisms), organic food, and the use of pesticides. Jack Granath, director of the Bonner Springs City Library, notes that members of the book club "include former farmers, a teacher of environmental science at a community college, and a master gardener, so lots of conversation comes out of inviting each one present to give a brief impression of the book."

A discussion of *The Omnivore's Dilemma: A Natural History of Four Meals* by Michael Pollan was one of the best in the group's history of meeting. Other successful titles have included *Prodigal Summer* by Barbara Kingsolver and *Combat-Ready Kitchen: How the U.S. Military Shapes the Way You Eat* by Anastacia Marx de Salcedo.

In addition to the usual library services, the Bonner Springs City Library "also runs the Bonner Springs Farmers Market and offers many related programs on gardening and cooking," says Granath. The library uses these events as well as its community ties to local clubs to promote its book club. While not every community will have access to some of the resources available in Bonner Springs, there may still be an interest in this type of book club. "Even though there are fewer and fewer farmers in America, there are lots of farmers' children and grandchildren out there, and they have memories of a vanishing world that they want to talk about," Granath says.

# Book and Pub Club

**VALLEY COTTAGE LIBRARY | VALLEY COTTAGE, NEW YORK**

**COMMUNITY TYPE: SUBURBAN**

When Katie Karkheck and Ashley Maraffino realized that their peers were not library users, they brainstormed ideas to appeal to the elusive twenty- and thirty-something crowd. The result was the Book and Pub Club, which has now been meeting in local bars and restaurants for five years. Karkheck, an adult services librarian at the Valley Cottage Library, elaborates on their success: "Over the last few years, we have earned a loyal following, where our participants have developed lasting friendships, have sometimes rediscovered a love of reading, and many have become avid library supporters and users."

During their first meeting, the group discussed *The Brief Wondrous Life of Oscar Wao* by Junot Díaz. To celebrate their one-year anniversary, the book club threw a birthday party complete with party hats, a birthday cake, and a discussion of a different novel by Díaz. *Dietland* by Sarai Walker was a memorable title, because the discussion led members to share their own personal experiences in a way they hadn't at previous meetings. Meg Wolitzer's *The Interestings* also struck a nerve with the group. Karkheck says: "It deals with how friendships change over time, how the things one is passionate about when younger can take a back burner to marriage, families, careers, etc., and how one's expectations of what adulthood looks like can be vastly different from reality." Every year during the summer months, the book club transforms into a summer school by rereading some classic titles they may have previously encountered in their high school English classes.

Partnerships with bars and restaurants as well as with the Nyack Library have enabled the staff to reach a much wider audience, while also bringing business to local establishments on weekday evenings. The benefits of their book club go beyond just encouraging members to read books and gather together in the community, though. As Karkheck notes, "We are there to encourage people to make new friends as much as to engage in an intellectual discussion."

## MARKETING TO THE ELUSIVE TWENTY- AND THIRTY-SOMETHINGS

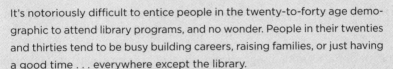

It's notoriously difficult to entice people in the twenty-to-forty age demographic to attend library programs, and no wonder. People in their twenties and thirties tend to be busy building careers, raising families, or just having a good time . . . everywhere except the library.

But don't give up—this age group can be reached, though you may need to change your approach. We found a handful of library workers who have successfully brought twenty- and thirty-somethings into their book clubs, and we asked them, "How did you do it?" Here's what they told us.

> "I really hit the town. I made a Meetup for it, did a Facebook event, and made a very attractive poster that prominently featured a lovely glass of craft beer. Most of the people that ended up coming in the beginning were 'library people' who had heard about it through the library, but they would bring a friend."
>
> —Leah LaFera, Read 'n' Greet Book Club,
> Schenectady County Public Library (book club no. 1)

> "I chose a place right off the public square, close to the university and a college movie theater, so there's a lot going on in that area. When we first started we used flyers, but we don't need them anymore. We get members through word of mouth, and we've been featured in *417* magazine and *Feast* magazine. We catch people's attention."
>
> —Konrad Stump, Donuts & Death, Springfield-Greene County Library
> (book club no. 41)

> "We thought online would be the best way to reach people in that age group. We did Meetups, Instagram posts, and we put up flyers at a local Starbucks and an area college that has a lot of nontraditional students who would be in the twenties and thirties age range."
>
> —Eileen Fontenot, Fine Liquorature Book Club,
> Thomas Crane Public Library (book club no. 5)

If all else fails, remember: there's no shame in dragging your friends, partner, and/or nieces and nephews along to the book club. We've all been there. ✄

# Alamance Social Justice Reading Group

**ALAMANCE COUNTY PUBLIC LIBRARIES | BURLINGTON, NORTH CAROLINA**
**COMMUNITY TYPE: URBAN**

An inspirational training program with the Racial Equity Institute led members of the community to found the Alamance Social Justice Reading Group. Katie DeVriese, a reference assistant at the Alamance County Public Libraries, says, "They wanted a space to delve more deeply into complex issues facing our society." The book club connects with local organizations that provide guidance in selecting the books, as well as guest speakers to lead the discussions.

The Social Justice Reading Group's monthly meetings usually begin with DeVriese asking participants about one thing from the book that surprised them or resonated with them in some way. This usually "sparks conversation, and participants are often engaged because of the subject matter of the books." DeVriese continues, "I usually try to have a representative from a community organization attend, when possible, since the participants are concerned about how issues affect us locally."

*Picking Cotton* by Jennifer Thompson-Cannino, Ronald Cotton, and Erin Torneo led to a particularly memorable meeting because the events in the book had actually occurred in Burlington in the 1980s. DeVriese recalls that the discussion was enhanced when one of the book club participants, "who was living here at the time, discussed the racial climate and how the court case and subsequent DNA exoneration affected the community." Other successful titles include *The New Jim Crow* by Michelle Alexander, *Evicted* by Matthew Desmond, and *Tattoos on the Heart* by Gregory Boyle. When discussing *Evicted*, DeVriese says the group "invited the director of a local homeless shelter who put into perspective poverty and homelessness in our community."

When selecting titles for discussion, the group is particularly mindful of representing a variety of perspectives. DeVriese stresses that "openness and understanding are key" to creating a similar type of book club in any community.

# Too Cool for School Book Club

**GWINNETT COUNTY PUBLIC LIBRARY | LAWRENCEVILLE, GEORGIA**
**COMMUNITY TYPE: SUBURBAN**

For years, the Gwinnett County Public Library had difficulty maintaining book clubs for children. "With several failures under our belt, we looked outside the system and discovered several homeschool groups in the area already organizing through social media. Instead of starting from scratch again and hoping to build a successful program, we established a relationship with the biggest group and offered them free space in the library to do their programs," says Don Giacomini, a youth services specialist. By working together, the homeschool group had assistance with advertising and logistics, and the library had a built-in audience for a book club.

Although the Too Cool for School Book Club is not actually run by staff, with thirty participants in the children's group and fifteen in the teen group, it is the library's most well-attended book club. The homeschool group is responsible for selecting the books, leading the discussion, and planning additional activities. Each month, the kids and teens meet in separate areas of the library. A mom of a homeschool student starts the children's group with a discussion and ends the meeting with activities that tie in to the themes of the book. When they read *Flower Moon* by Gina Linko, Giacomini recalls that they "spent a good deal of time talking about the things that pull us together and push us apart." The group followed that discussion by making magnetic slime and investigating the strengths of a variety of magnets.

On the other side of the library, the teen group operates much like any other book club. After a discussion of the book, they generally spend the rest of the meeting socializing. While they might play games or talk about other books and movies they like, Giacomini notes that if the book is popular, the teens "keep talking until their parents drag them out."

CHAPTER THREE

# UNITE PEOPLE WITH COMMON INTERESTS

**B**ook clubs center around discussions. But when members are shy or reluctant to share with the group, it can be difficult to facilitate a meeting. The easiest way to ensure that a book club will always have something to talk about is to bring people together who share a common interest. Most people enjoy talking about their hobbies or a topic that excites them, even if they are not comfortable divulging a lot of personal information.

It is up to the facilitator to decide if that shared interest will be a method for selecting books, an activity to do during meetings, or a combination of both. Whatever the subject that links members, discussions will be richer and easier to facilitate if there is a bit of common ground.

# Knitters Book Club

**JONATHAN BOURNE PUBLIC LIBRARY | BOURNE, MASSACHUSETTS**

**COMMUNITY TYPE: RURAL**

While the Knitters Book Club began for people who enjoyed both knitting and reading, it has since become open to people who prefer other sorts of crafts, as well as people who just want to hear what other members think about books. "We have found that sometimes the camaraderie is more important than the book, but it always goes back to what we are reading and how the stories impact our own lives," says Diane Ranney, assistant director at the Jonathan Bourne Public Library.

While it can be hard to keep the conversation from wandering off topic, one benefit of ten years together is that the members often feel more comfortable sharing their personal stories with the group. After reading a novel about abuse, one of the women opened up about her experience. "All of the members present that evening were so compassionate and offered the gift of just listening to her. No advice was given, just the time to let her share her experience and then talk about how difficult it is for women to be able to do that," recalls Ranney.

*Lillian Boxfish Takes a Walk* by Kathleen Rooney also led to an interesting discussion. Ranney says the novel "reminded us all of times in our lives when we either regretted something we had done or regretted something we had not done." Additionally, the book emphasized that great things can be accomplished at any age, inspiring the members over forty to think about what they might still want to do in their lifetime. Most of the members enjoyed the first *Maisie Dobbs* novel by Jacqueline Winspear as well, but when Ranney asked why someone was not a fan, they remarked, "Now, I have to read all fourteen of them!"

The Knitters Book Club learned to always be in attendance for whatever book you select after a disastrous reading of Candice Millard's *The River of Doubt.* Ranney says they now have a regular saying if an unpopular book is selected: "Well, at least it isn't as bad as *River of Doubt.*"

# Bushwick Book Club Seattle

**BUSHWICK NORTHWEST | SEATTLE, WASHINGTON**
**COMMUNITY TYPE: URBAN**

Almost every month, you can find members of the Bushwick Book Club Seattle performing music inspired by a particular book. Bushwick Northwest, a non-profit organization, has been running the group for eight years "to create vibrant programming and support musicians, authors, and our audience," says Geoff Larson, the organization's executive director.

After reading a book agreed upon by both the organization's Book Selection Committee and the Advisory Board, the members each write their own piece of music and gather at libraries, music venues, theaters, or other places to perform in front of an audience. Because writing is a very personal process, members work on their music separately. When describing his writing process, Larson says, "I often build a whole song around a phrase I think is catchy and resonates with my feelings surrounding the book." Each performance consists of about ten different musicians sharing their music with an audience that may or may not have read the book. The members then discuss the book on stage, allowing for audience participation.

The Bushwick Book Club first performed in October 2010. Kurt Vonnegut's novel *Slaughterhouse-Five* was the inspiration for this event, and the reaction from both the audience and the musicians was encouraging. Other memorable events have centered around Octavia Butler's *Parable of the Sower* and Cheryl Strayed's *Wild*. The latter performance took place in front of an audience of 2,500 that included the book's author.

Larson notes that their "struggles come from the growing pains of a nonprofit organization." Learning how to work within financial constraints and developing partnerships with musicians who already have ties in the community have helped the group continue to put on successful events. Larson says the group hopes people who attend their performances have "an open mind about bringing a variety of art forms together in the name of creating new works."

# President's Book Club

**IDYLLWILD LIBRARY, RIVERSIDE COUNTY LIBRARY SYSTEM**

**IDYLLWILD, CALIFORNIA**

**COMMUNITY TYPE: RURAL**

When the President's Book Club began meeting in February 2016, "the goal was to learn about our presidential history during a time of what seemed to be great divisiveness in the current political climate," says the club's coordinator, Colleen Tell. The first meeting—where members discussed *Washington: A Life* by Ron Chernow—was one of their best. Tell says the book gave everyone "a great understanding of events leading up to the creation of our country and our government."

For the last two years, the group has met every other month to discuss a different president, in the order in which they served. Rather than read a specific title, each member selects a book, Internet resource, or documentary relevant to the president's time in office. During each discussion, Shannon Ng, branch manager at the Idyllwild Library, says the members consider the following questions: "What makes a good president? What political conflicts occurred specific to their term(s)? What can American history tell us about the times we live in today?" While members enjoy the freedom of selecting their own materials, the book club has discovered a lack of information available about some of the past presidents and the events that occurred during their terms.

The members of the President's Book Club are generally respectful of each other and tend to stick to discussing facts and events, but differing opinions can sometimes cause tension within the group. Tell recalls that during one meeting, "a Republican and a Democrat in our group worked up into a heated argument over Andrew Jackson and his associates." Regardless of personal opinions or political beliefs, Tell says all of the members "have found it fascinating to uncover or rediscover historical events that have shaped our nation."

## Running and Reading

**RYE PUBLIC LIBRARY | RYE, NEW HAMPSHIRE**
COMMUNITY TYPE: SMALL TOWN

The popularity of Christopher McDougall's *Born to Run* led to the first six-week session of the Running and Reading Book Club. Andrew Richmond, director of the Rye Public Library, says that each session has been "timed to coincide with local races so the group can train and then race together if they choose." Both beginners and seasoned runners are encouraged to join the group. "During our first session, one member trained and ran a first 5K race, while another finished the session with a marathon," notes Richmond.

When the group is in session, the meetings begin each week with a traditional book club discussion within the walls of the library, and end with a run out in the community. One challenge with this active book club is beginning the evening meetings at a time that provides enough daylight to accommodate both a book discussion and a run. Richmond says that planning the week's discussion also requires staff to think carefully, because the "questions must refer to designated chapters and not reveal future events [in the book]." Most of the discussion questions found online address a book as a whole, so staff have to either edit the questions to reflect that week's selection or write their own questions entirely. In addition to weekly meetings, an e-mail newsletter that includes information about cultures or foods mentioned in the book, as well as a preview of the next week's questions, is sent out to all members.

While all of the selected titles focus on the topic of running, the group has read both fiction and nonfiction books. Members particularly enjoyed reading *Running the Rift* by Naomi Benaron and *Run the World: My 3,500-Mile Journey through Running Cultures around the Globe* by Becky Wade. After reading *Run the World*, they had a memorable Skype discussion with the author.

## Mysteries Around the World

**STARR LIBRARY | RHINEBECK, NEW YORK**

**COMMUNITY TYPE: RURAL**

Program coordinator Nan Jackson knew there were already several mystery book clubs in her community of Rhinebeck, New York. To stand out, she knew her library needed a mystery book club with a twist. Her brainstorming sessions led to the creation of Mysteries Around the World, a book club for "adult mystery buffs and people interested in different cultures."

Each month, the group reads a mystery from a different country. While Jackson prepares information about the author and the book in advance, the book club otherwise runs smoothly without much intervention from her. She says the members enjoy "comparing detectives, culture, food (in many of the books there are great descriptions of food), and the actual approach to detective work."

As with any book club, selecting titles can be challenging, particularly when the book club leader is not actually a fan of mystery novels. Thankfully, the collective knowledge of the book club members has helped with the selection process. Additionally, Jackson often suggests that the group try the first book in a series. As she notes, "It's encouraging when our detective buffs plan to continue with the series." Some of the titles that members have enjoyed include *Wife of the Gods* by Kwei Quartey, *Finding Nouf* by Zoë Ferraris, and *Faceless Killers* by Henning Mankell. Set in Ghana, Saudi Arabia, and Sweden, respectively, each book offered opportunities for dynamic discussions about rituals, gender, and immigration.

Jackson offers one piece of advice to anyone wishing to start a similar book club in their community: "Enjoy the ride. It's marvelous to be searching for clues in the French Dordogne one month and on the jagged shores of Australia the next."

## Quintessential Sequential Book Club

**ALBANY COUNTY PUBLIC LIBRARY | LARAMIE, WYOMING**

COMMUNITY TYPE: RURAL

Tyler Brown, an adult services specialist at the Albany County Public Library, says the Quintessential Sequential Book Club is "a place for interested newcomers and fans of the sequential art form of literature (graphic novels, comic books, manga, etc.) to discover and discuss all the beautiful, provocative, and heroic stories the form has to offer." Although anyone sixteen or older is invited to attend the meetings, most of the members are in their twenties.

The group gathers every month at the Rib and Chop House of Wyoming, a restaurant in the community. Brown says, "The manager of the restaurant is an avid comic book reader and he provides us with lots of tasty appetizers." When selecting books, Brown notifies members in advance if there are any topics that might be upsetting. Attendance varies from month to month, as some people choose not to read particular titles, but the majority of the members are open to at least trying to read every book.

Brown notes that *Motor Girl* by Terry Moore, *Saga, Vol 1* by Brian K. Vaughan, and *From Hell* by Alan Moore were "all successful for different reasons, but mainly they all led to incredible discussions about the art form, with the story and emotional impacts—or lack thereof—generating the most interesting discussions, regardless of being loved or hated by members of the group." Even unpopular books have led to great discussions. When a book was disliked by all but one member, Brown recalls, "we sat and debated it for a long while and by the end of the discussion, opinions had shifted and members began to understand others' perspectives and even began to see beauty in the book."

Brown's advice for starting a graphic novel book club is simple: "Do it. Graphic novels have always been a point of discussion, and now more than ever they are in the public consciousness."

# Once Upon a Time Book Club

**DELTA COMMUNITY LIBRARY | DELTA JUNCTION, ALASKA**

**COMMUNITY TYPE: RURAL**

When most people think about picture books, they probably imagine young children flipping through the pages of a favorite story with a parent or grandparent. However, for the members of the Once Upon a Time Book Club, picture books are the ideal literature for an enthusiastic discussion among adults.

Every month, adults eighteen and older meet in the children's area of the Delta Community Library to read a picture book and discuss the text and illustrations. After the meeting, the club donates a copy of the book to the library. The group's most successful titles have included *The Bedspread* by Sylvia Fair, *That's Good! That's Bad!* by Marjorie Cuyler, and *Tops & Bottoms* by Janet Stevens. All three books led to animated conversations among the members in attendance. For library director Joyce McCombs, "It's really fun to hear adults get excited about kids' books in the first place, and then to hear them be happy that kids will be enjoying the books that are donated to the library."

For anyone wishing to facilitate a similar book group, McCombs recommends that staff prepare questions in advance, but let the group navigate the discussion, only interjecting if the conversation stalls. She also suggests providing a tasty treat at every meeting.

McCombs says the book club's only bump in the road so far "was an area-wide power failure! We had 80 mph winds and no power for 16 hours in town." Unfortunately, the book club was not able to meet that month due to these extreme conditions. Weather is often an issue for this town. "We are at the end of the Alaska Highway in Delta Junction and 100 miles from a major town (Fairbanks)," McCombs says. "Creating our own diversions is essential to surviving winters at –50 below . . . and some years, even colder."

# CHAPTER FOUR

# MAKE IT EASY
# FOR THEM

**I**t's hard to get consistent attendance at book clubs. You may have tried changing the meeting time or moving the meetings to a different location, with little or no success. Putting on any program takes time, but with a book club, you are also spending hours reading the selected title, making it all the more frustrating when no one shows up at your meeting.

For our patrons, joining a book club is a big commitment. In addition to attending meetings once a month, they have to devote time from their busy lives to get through the book. In this chapter, you will see examples of how libraries are making it easy to participate in book clubs by really considering the needs of their patrons when designing the format.

# BYOBOOKS Dessert Discussion Group

**MORRISTOWN CENTENNIAL LIBRARY | MORRISVILLE, VERMONT**
**COMMUNITY TYPE: RURAL**

The BYOBOOKS Dessert Discussion Group combines two elements—a no-assigned-reading book club and a dessert potluck—to create a one-of-a-kind group. What began in 2015 as a special summer program series quickly became a full-fledged book group when the members decided they liked meeting too much to limit their discussions to the summer months. The ten regular book club members, women ranging in age from their mid-twenties to their early nineties, get together every month to discuss books and participate in a competitive potluck in hopes of winning the coveted Most Delicious on the Table award.

Because members are allowed to choose their own books, this program is largely patron-driven. They decide how many books they want to read and discuss in a month, and they lead the conversation. Gizelle Guyette, director of the Morristown Centennial Library, thinks this format "is a good way to allow avid readers and scholars in the community to offer their expertise."

Members are encouraged to review up to three titles of their choice every month. After the meeting, library staff compile the reviews into a magazine that is regularly sought out by the wider library community. For Guyette, "the beauty—and fun—of this group is that the members select whatever they want to highlight. We're all adults, and although our political, philosophical, and religious creeds and world views differ, we can (usually) discuss it peacefully. Some will love a book and others loathe it, and the party line is that 'This is a book discussion, not a book agreement. There is room for dissent.'"

Although they don't all read the same book, there tend to be trends in the reading material. Some popular authors have included Louise Penny, Chris Bohjalian, Anne Lamott, Bill Bryson, and Mary Oliver. Guyette says the members have also "gotten more into youth literature, sharing some of those beautiful picture books that are too glorious to be reserved just for children."

# Low Maintenance Book Club

**DUKE UNIVERSITY LIBRARIES | DURHAM, NORTH CAROLINA**
**COMMUNITY TYPE: URBAN**

Duke University Libraries has found a creative way to make book club membership less demanding for members with the Low Maintenance Book Club. Meeting monthly, the club's members—students, faculty, and other members of the university community—discuss pieces that can be read in less than thirty minutes, since many of their members are conducting research or are reading materials assigned in their classes.

Often with library programs, there is a tendency to measure success by the number of patrons who attend a program. However, Arianne Hartsell-Gundy, a librarian for literature and theater studies at Duke University Libraries, determines the success of her Low Maintenance Book Club "not just by attendance numbers, but also by the depth of discussion the work generates. Works that are more controversial or open to interpretation have led to very thoughtful and interesting exchanges."

Two of their most successful discussions centered around *The Story of Your Life* by Ted Chiang and selections from *Citizen: An American Lyric* by Claudia Rankin. While discussing *The Story of Your Life*, a linguist and a physicist in attendance ended up with a large, unplanned role in that month's meeting. "They led a fascinating discussion on the nature of time and the link between language and cognition. Both participants were able to fully relate their academic background to the work," Hartsell-Gundy says. When the group discussed *Citizen*, the conversation turned to some of the topics addressed in the work like racial violence, discrimination, and microaggressions. "We were surprised at the level of discussion from the undergraduates at that meeting and how deeply they engaged with the work and with others in the discussion," Hartsell-Gundy notes.

As with any book club, not every selection has been a hit, such as an attempt to introduce the group to Westerns. Hartsell-Gundy tries to be "mindful of representing a diversity of authors and genres." She also looks to the members of the Low Maintenance Book Club for recommendations.

# Books & Bites

**BENTONVILLE PUBLIC LIBRARY | BENTONVILLE, ARKANSAS**
**COMMUNITY TYPE: SUBURBAN**

In March 2017, the Bentonville Public Library in Arkansas started circulating Books & Bites Book Club Kits. Senior librarian Courtney Fitzgerald says the kits were created "to provide a cost-effective way for members of our community to host a book club-themed event in the comfort of their own home, without the hassle of conducting the research themselves or purchasing books individually each month."

Each kit contains ten copies of the book, information about the book and author, discussion questions, a list of similar titles, and a copy of the movie adaptation, if applicable. A planning guide called the Snacks & Sips menu is also enclosed. Fitzgerald notes: "The menu includes themed appetizers and beverages that tie into the storyline or are mentioned in the story, and decorations applicable to the story to provide a comprehensive themed event experience."

Since the kits have been added to the collection, they have circulated sixty-four times. The three highest-circulating kits have been *A Man Called Ove* by Fredrik Backman, *Big Little Lies* by Liane Moriarty, and *The Husband's Secret* by Liane Moriarty. Books are selected based on their high circulation or their success in the library's regular book clubs. Patron suggestions are also considered.

The library circulates kits for children and teens as well. These kits are identical to the adult kits, but Fitzgerald says they also feature "a Games & Grubs menu, which includes recipes for easy-to-make snacks for all attendees, as well as multiple games everyone can play that are applicable to the story." Although they have not been as popular as the adult kits, circulation has increased after staff moved the kits to the youth department.

While the kits were designed for patrons, some library staff have been utilizing them as well. A librarian from a nearby library regularly borrows the kits because her library's limited budget is unable to fund an adult book club. Fitzgerald says, "Her library is in a rural community, and the kits have helped bring neighbors together over a book club."

## Open Book Club

**CALIMESA LIBRARY, RIVERSIDE COUNTY LIBRARY SYSTEM**

**CALIMESA, CALIFORNIA**

COMMUNITY TYPE: RURAL

The Calimesa Library used to have a Mystery Book Club. Despite promoting the book group everywhere they could, they only ever had two or three people attend every month. Eventually, they decided that if attendance didn't approve, they would have to discontinue the book club.

As a last attempt, the library decided to make it easier for members to participate. They changed the club's name to the Open Book Club, eliminated any required reading, and called on current members to help recruit new members. "We were so reluctant to give a deadline for growth, but it ended up being the best decision we could have made," says the branch manager, Alyson Hamlin.

The Open Book Club has now been meeting for over two years. Members can read whichever title they'd like every month. Hamlin says, "Each person shows up with a summary prepared, as well as a 'teaser' that is just a few lines." At the end of the meeting, staff collect all the teasers and create a bookmark with the club's recommendations. The finished bookmark is then available for all library patrons to pick up at the front desk.

While members are free to choose books from any genre, mystery, science fiction, and fantasy novels are the most popular. Rather than have a staff member lead the group, the Open Book Club is run by a volunteer who occasionally asks questions to keep the discussion going. For smaller libraries, finding a volunteer to run a book club is a great way to continue offering a long-running program even when other demands are placed on the staff.

Prior to starting a new book club, try finding a few interested community members who will also help promote the group to all their friends. As Hamlin says, "a book club is often a social affair, and people seem more likely to attend when their friends are going."

## THE RIGHT SIZE

There is no magic number of attendees that makes a book club a success. LitLovers, an online book club resource, recommends eight to sixteen members. In *The Librarian's Guide to Book Programs and Author Events*, Brad Hooper argues that there is a sweet spot between ten and twenty members; above that, Hooper says, the club should be closed off to new members until spaces open up.

But this doesn't mean that clubs with smaller groups are doomed to fail. Countless book clubs thrive with just a few dedicated members, especially those that read books about niche topics, or ones that are located in small or rural communities. In fact, BookBrowse.com estimates that 60 percent of in-person book clubs have ten or fewer members.

In fact, larger clubs come with their own problems, as people get less time to contribute in large groups, often leaving a few outgoing folks to dominate the conversation and making meaningful connections difficult.

Instead of counting heads, try judging your success based on the quality of the conversation. "I gauge how successful a discussion is by the following criteria: Do I have to cut the discussion short because the waitstaff want to go home and we are all still talking?" says Leah LaFera, founder of the Read 'n' Greet Book Club (book club no. 1) at the Schenectady County Public Library.

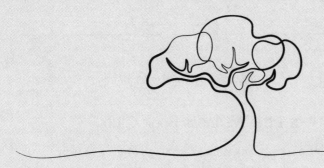

# CHAPTER FIVE

# MEET A NEED

B ook clubs are fun, but they can also serve important purposes in both the community and the library—from social opportunities for isolated segments of the population, to valuable skills-building for those in need, to providing a strategic way to advance your library's mission.

If your book club is struggling, take a step back and consider: are you giving your patrons what they need? Or an even better starting question: do you actually *know* what your patrons need? If not, start asking questions and find out—and then consider how a book club could help fill the gap.

## Quality of Life Wellness Book Club

**INDIANAPOLIS PUBLIC LIBRARY, EAST 38TH STREET BRANCH**

**INDIANAPOLIS, INDIANA**

COMMUNITY TYPE: URBAN

Food insecurity is a problem for many Indianapolis residents, especially those living on the city's east side. WalkScore.com ranked Indianapolis last among major U.S. cities in 2016 for access to healthy foods, noting that only 5 percent of residents live within a five-minute walk of a grocery store. According to Feeding America, a network of hunger relief organizations, nearly 20 percent of the population of Marion County, in which Indianapolis is located, faces food insecurity.

The Indianapolis Public Library, in partnership with the Indianapolis Urban League, has found a way to help fight these problems with the Quality of Life Wellness Book Club, a group that strives to ignite conversations about health and instill healthy habits in residents.

"Our community is a food desert—there's no grocery store with healthy food within walking distance of the East 38th Street Branch," says librarian Shanika Heyward, the book club's creator. "We started this club in 2016 as a way to get our patrons reading and also to help them make healthier choices. Because you can read about health and wellness all day, but if you don't practice it, it does no good."

In each two-hour meeting, participants gather at the library to discuss a chapter from a book like *Grain Brain: The Surprising Truth about Wheat, Carbs, and Sugar* by David Perlmutter, or *Salt Sugar Fat: How the Food Giants Hooked Us* by Michael Moss. Each member starts by introducing herself and sharing something she learned from the chapter and how she applied that new recommendation, skill, or concept in her life.

After the discussion, an Urban League wellness coach demonstrates how to cook a simple dish, such as a vegetable quinoa bowl, that is made with organic produce from the League's gardens. Everyone gets to sample the recipe, and then the coach leads them through some simple exercises and stretches. The group has also gone grocery-shopping together.

Attendance at the club's meetings ranges from ten to twenty attendees, and Heyward credits the strong turnout to word of mouth. "If you're excited about your book club, you're going to invite everybody under the sun to come with you," she says. "It's like a good support group."

The trick to creating a book club that meets your community's needs is to ask people what they want, Heyward says. "Get out of the library building and learn what's important to the community," she says. "If I never go out and meet my community and find out what's important to them, how can I offer what they need?"

## Large Print Book Club

**CAMPBELL COUNTY PUBLIC LIBRARY | GILLETTE, WYOMING**
**COMMUNITY TYPE: RURAL**

When the Campbell County Public Library was looking for a new way to engage its community's sizable senior population, the library's Adult Programming Committee floated the idea of a Large Print Book Club. "We guessed that there was a need for this kind of program," says Nancy Venable, the library's extension and volunteer services manager. "And we got a great response, so we were correct."

The library now leads six different Large Print Book Clubs at Gillette's senior center and at various retirement communities around town. Each club has its own assigned reading, so people often attend more than one club per month. The library staff create author biographies and discussion sheets for each title, and distribute them to book club members when they receive their books.

While the clubs are popular now, they required a lot of groundwork to get up and running. Each retirement community has its own culture; while a book club may be a hit in one residence, another may prefer shopping outings or other activities. Campbell County Public Library staff relied on surveys and personal contacts at the facilities to determine which locations would be a good fit. "Also, be open to a change in location," Venable says. "We moved one meeting location to a complex half a block up the street and tripled the attendance in two months."

Even if you do your research and find a senior community that is a good fit, your turnout may be small to start with. Retirement community residents were hesitant to give the Large Print Book Club a chance at first, and it took word of mouth to get them to come. "They basically sent in a spy to see what the book club was like," Venable says. "When the spy reported back that it was okay, we would get four more people the next week."

Logistically, it can be disappointing when a desired book club title isn't available in large print, but "it's gotten so much better," Venable says. Distributors like Center Point Large Print and Thorndike Press Large Print carry most of the books the Large Print Book Club has wanted, although Venable warns that they are often pricier than the regular format.

## Brown Bag Lunch Club

**JOHNSON COUNTY LIBRARY | BUFFALO, WYOMING**

**COMMUNITY TYPE: RURAL**

The long, frigid winters of northern Wyoming can challenge even the most weather-hardened residents in the town of Buffalo. So in 2017, the Johnson County Library set out to create an event that would give their patrons a reason to get out of the house in the dreary winter months: an adult storytime.

The Brown Bag Lunch Club is a weekly reading club, with meetings from October to April, in which local authors and library staff read aloud to an audience in a library meeting room. The selections are typically adult books—local history is especially popular—though occasionally, a children's librarian has brought in a kids' title for her turn to read. A different book is featured every week, so listeners only get to hear a snippet of each title, although they are encouraged to check out the books to finish reading at home, and many do.

"We've read all different genres—poetry, history, science fiction," says Nancy Tabb, the library's local history and interlibrary loan librarian. "People like the fact that we read books they might not have picked up on their own." Popular titles have included *The Life and Adventures of Frank Grouard* by Joe De Barthe, a historical account first published in 1894 about a champion U.S. Army scout; and *Sagebrush Dentist* as told by Will Frackelton to Herman Gastrell Seely, a Western novel set in Wyoming. Members listen to the reading while they eat, and then take part in a discussion. (The food is brown-bag style, though the library does put out a small spread of coffee and candy.)

The Brown Bag Lunch Club gatherings have attracted as many as 30 people per session—a solid turnout in a community of 4,500. The audience is mixed: about half are workers visiting the library on their lunch breaks, and half are retirees or residents of area nursing homes, who come as a group.

Library staff have been surprised at how successful the series has been. "When we first started the series, we thought, 'We'll give it a try,'" Tabb says. "We've been very impressed. People get here ten minutes early with their lunches, waiting to get started." Some adults have even asked if they could bring along their children; however, the library decided to keep the program for adults only.

## Read More! Book Club

**SEYMOUR PUBLIC LIBRARY DISTRICT | AUBURN, NEW YORK**
**COMMUNITY TYPE: SMALL CITY**

The Seymour Public Library District started the Read More! Book Club to meet a library need rather than a community need: getting people to take part in a new reading challenge.

Before Read More! the library hosted a traditional book club for about a decade, but attendance dropped steadily over the years. "We tried changing the meeting day and time but didn't see much change in attendance—sometimes it would be down to me and one other person," says library director Lisa Carr. So in 2016, when the library introduced a new reading challenge, they decided to recast the struggling book club to support the goals of the challenge.

The Read More! 2018 Reading Challenge invited patrons to read twenty-six books throughout the year that fit into different reading categories—for example, a book with an appealing cover, a novel based on a real person, and a book with song lyrics in the title. The affiliated book club, which met on Wednesday evenings, gave readers a fun, social way to stay on track to complete the challenge.

Each month's meeting was designed not around a single title, but around one of the challenge's themes. Members may read any book they like that fits the criteria. "A big part of our discussion is why they picked that particular book," Carr says, "which leads to some interesting conversations." A library staffer kicks off the discussion by introducing the chosen category and sharing information about library resources, including how patrons can find books to read for the challenge.

When the Seymour Public Library District created the Read More! Book Club, they also moved its meetings to a local brewpub. The new location is a boon for some members. "It's a hot spot in town," Carr says. "We know all the waitstaff and they know us, so that's kind of fun." The noise level has been a challenge, so as a backup, the group has occasionally relocated to a bakery next door, and they plan to try out a new coffee shop as well.

# Low Vision Readers Book Group

**SEATTLE PUBLIC LIBRARY | SEATTLE, WASHINGTON**
**COMMUNITY TYPE: URBAN**

In 2006, a Seattle-area low vision support group came to their public library with a request. The group's eighteen members, who met at a local hospital, wanted to stay active and to keep doing things they enjoyed despite their visual disabilities—and that included reading. Would the library host a book club for them, they asked?

"I said, 'Oh, definitely,'" recalls Cleo Brooks, ADA coordinator and supervising librarian of the Seattle Public Library's Library Equal Access Program, and so the Low Vision Readers Book Group was born. Years later, the group continues to attract 15 to 25 members to its monthly meetings. Most attend in person, with some utilizing the county's accessible public transit options to get to the library's Central Location in downtown Seattle; others, including those who have moved out of state or have limited mobility, dial in via a conference phone line.

With members reading several different formats, it was an "evolution" to get the books that everyone needed, Brooks says. Most book club members are also affiliated with the Washington Talking Book and Braille Library, a program of the Washington State Library, and receive audiobook copies of their book club selections through that organization. Some members who are low-vision, as opposed to completely blind, prefer to read large-print format books, and others download their materials digitally via Overdrive, so the club always selects books that are accessible to all of its members. One member, who is deaf, periodically joins, reading standard-format print books and attending the group with an interpreter.

The book club discussions are facilitated by one of three book club volunteers, each of whom is blind; the facilitators, like all library volunteers, are required to take part in a library training. Book recommendations frequently come from members' recommendations. Favorites have included *A Man Called Ove* by Fredrick Backman, *The Immortal Life of Henrietta Lacks* by Rebecca Skloot, and *The Good Earth* by Pearl S. Buck. "The book club participants are lively and definitely not shy about respectfully sharing their opinions," Brooks says. "It's never hard to engage this group."

## Healthy Exchange Book Club

**BRAINERD MEMORIAL LIBRARY | HADDAM, CONNECTICUT**
**COMMUNITY TYPE: SUBURBAN**

When Sue Staehly was diagnosed with breast cancer in 2010, she threw herself into healthy eating and general wellness as a way to ensure a healthier future. "I became a real fanatic," recalls Staehly, who is technical services coordinator at the Brainerd Memorial Library. "I had 30 or 40 books checked out at a time, mainly on disease prevention and how to stay healthy going forward."

When a coworker was also diagnosed with the disease, the two formed an informal gathering for women facing cancer. While that group, called The Sisterhood, eventually disbanded, its success inspired Staehly to broaden the group's scope and make it an official book club at her library. The Healthy Exchange Book Club began reading and participating in healthy activities together in 2013.

For nine months of the year, on Wednesday evenings, members of the Healthy Exchange read nonfiction books on health and wellness topics. Selections have included *Mind Over Meds* by Andrew Weil, *Braving the Wilderness: The Quest for True Belonging and the Courage to Stand Alone* by Brené Brown, and *Real Food/ Fake Food: Why You Don't Know What You're Eating and What You Can Do About It* by Larry Olmsted. On occasion, the group will read and discuss books about illnesses, such as Alzheimer's or Parkinson's, that are affecting book club members or their loved ones. "These are topics that our members are struggling with," Staehly says, "so we provide an opportunity to learn about it together."

In the summer months, the Healthy Exchange Book Club takes a break from reading to focus on health-related activities. In 2018 they played pickleball, went paddle-boarding, and played mini-golf; their past activities have included zip lining, tubing on the Farmington River, belly dancing, and crystal bowl sound healing. "I like to do anything, just to give people a new experience," Staehly says. In December, members meet for dinner at a health-conscious restaurant, where the reading list for the coming year—which members vote on each November—is unveiled.

# Oasis Book Club

**OASIS COALITION OF BOSTON | BOSTON, MASSACHUSETTS**
**COMMUNITY TYPE: URBAN**

When Peter Resnik and Rob Day struck up a conversation about sports one morning more than a decade ago, they had no way of knowing that it would lead to a long-standing book club for people experiencing homelessness in Boston. But Resnik, an attorney, and Day, a homeless veteran who was then spending his nights in Boston Common, soon found that they had more to talk about than the New England Patriots: they both had a love of literature.

"I gave Rob a book called *Water for Elephants*, which we would talk about on the way to work," Resnik told an NPR reporter in 2010. "And then we started on another book, and I asked him what he had done with *Water for Elephants*, and he had given it to someone else on the common. And I asked what they did with it, and they had given it to someone else."

Confident that there was interest in a book club for people experiencing homelessness in Boston, they found a church, Church on the Hill, that was willing to host weekly gatherings—and the Oasis Book Club still meets there today. "We meet once a week, no matter what," says Jenifer Whitmore, a volunteer who now manages the club. "It could be three people reading, it could be twelve people reading, but we're there. I feel like everyone has tailored their week around this group."

The group covers a wide range of genres. "We've read stories based in Boston, historical fiction, nonfiction—bring it, we'll read it," Whitmore says. Some of the club's books are donated by authors or by other local book clubs that donate their used books. The meeting format is free-form, and the club typically spends several weeks on a single book. If everyone has read the book, they will discuss it; other times, they will sit together and read a chapter aloud. Members may keep the books when they are finished.

To start a book club for people experiencing homelessness, start by reaching out to organizers in your community who are already working with the population, the Oasis Book Club creators say. This will help establish a core group of attendees and provide insight into logistics like location and book selection. A library is an ideal spot, they say, especially if it is already frequented by homeless people; shelters, drop-in centers, and churches are also good choices. Whitmore also suggests using paperbacks, since they are lighter for readers to carry.

Whitmore says that while the Oasis Book Club is about fostering a love of books, it's also about providing community to people who have become marginalized. "A homeless person may have lost their place, their standing. But if you ask, they may be very well informed on current event, sports, politics," she says. "They may be more well-read than you are."

## Next Chapter Book Club

**SCOTCH PLAINS PUBLIC LIBRARY | SCOTCH PLAINS, NEW JERSEY**

**COMMUNITY TYPE: SUBURBAN**

In 2007, a Scotch Plains Public Library board member came to Pam Brooks and asked about starting a book club for her son, who was developmentally disabled. "I didn't know where to start," recalls Brooks, the library's head of adult services. "I came from a special libraries background—I had never run a book club, let alone a book club for people with developmental disabilities. But I went to my computer, and she went to hers, and we came up with the Next Chapter Book Club."

The Next Chapter Book Club is a book club program for teens and adults with Down syndrome, autism, cerebral palsy, and other intellectual and developmental disabilities. The organization was founded in 2002 by Thomas Fish, director of Ohio State University's Nisonger Center for Excellence in Disabilities; today, there are 250 Next Chapter clubs throughout the United States, with more in Canada, Australia, Britain, and Germany. Next Chapter hosts pay a one-time fee of $350 for online training and access to a portal with resources and activities.

Next Chapter suggests that clubs meet weekly in a public space, such as a coffee shop, and read the books aloud as a group. Facilitators are encouraged to keep the conversation flowing, and not to get bogged down by trying to teach reading skills. "The idea is simple: let people be people and enjoy one another's company," Fish says. "It's a way for people with disabilities to have a chance to be genuinely and authentically part of their community."

Brooks quickly learned that there was no reason to worry about running a book club for people with disabilities. The teen book club she started in 2007 has continued; today, she has two Next Chapter clubs that meet back-to-back on Tuesday evenings at a local Panera Bread café. "Everyone has a copy of the book, we each read a page or two, pass it on to the next person, have a snack, talk about our week, and that's that," Brooks says. Favorite books have included

*Charlie and the Chocolate Factory* by Roald Dahl, *Rooftoppers* by Katherine Rundell, and Carl Hiaasen's books for young adults.

Each gathering starts with time for socializing, with everyone getting the chance to share updates about their week. It's a time for meaningful connection, especially as people age out of services. "They leave school and suddenly, they're isolated. But they know once a week, we will be there," Brooks says.

As for the hosts? "It's wonderful. It's life-affirming. It makes you feel really good about being a librarian."

## Autism Society of Minnesota Book Club

### DAKOTA COUNTY LIBRARY | EAGAN, MINNESOTA
#### COMMUNITY TYPE: SUBURBAN

When the Dakota County Library received a grant from the Minnesota Department of Human Services to serve people with autism, staff knew they wanted to make the library more welcoming for people on the autism spectrum. But they didn't know what that program would look like until the grant brought them together with the folks from AuSM.

The Autism Society of Minnesota, or AuSM (pronounced "awesome"), had noticed a common thread among their constituents. "When people registered for our activities, we would ask about their interests, and we saw 'reading' again and again," says Robyn DeCourcy, AuSM's education program specialist. "People with autism also tell us that reading helps them calm down and self-regulate when they get upset."

AuSM connected the library with a facilitator, a local special education teacher experienced at working with people with autism, and in August 2017, the AuSM Book Club began. While the club is open to anyone, it is designed for people with autism or other disabilities aged fourteen and older—mainly adolescents and young adults who are learning to live more independently. The readers come alone, without parents or caretakers. "We want them to talk and have a voice," says Renee Grassi, the library's youth services manager. "I've seen individuals blossom as their parents or caretakers leave, since they feel they can speak for themselves and share their opinions."

At first, organizers tried having all the members read the same book, mainly novels for young readers like *The One and Only Ivan* by K. A. Applegate and *Wonder* by R. J. Palacio. But they soon realized that this typical model wasn't meeting members' needs. "The books were too high-level for some readers, too low-level for others," Grassi says. "We decided to try something else."

Under the current format, meetings are part book discussion and part book selection. Members vote at the beginning of the school year on a list of genres to read each month; readers can pick any title they like. Each monthly meeting begins with an informal chat, giving readers time to connect. Then they begin the book discussion, with each person sharing five things about their book that they liked, didn't like, or learned.

Finally, the group splits up, and members work with the facilitator or library staff to select their books for the next month. "We sit down one-on-one with the individuals and ask what they like, look at the computer catalog together, and help them find the book on the shelves," Grassi says. "We are teaching valuable information literacy skills, and also getting them familiar with the library and its people."

The club is also important for the social network it creates, DeCourcy says. "To have a place in the community where they can go and be themselves—that kind of thing is pretty rare for some of our folks."

# CHAPTER SIX

# TARGET YOUR AUDIENCE

**I**t may seem safest to offer a book club that appeals to large swaths of the population—if we want to reach more people, you may reason, why would we want to exclude anyone?

Ironically, sometimes you can be more effective by narrowing your focus. Creating a book club for a specific group of people (think: nurses, city employees, special education teachers, opera enthusiasts) can enable you to read books on shared interests, form richer bonds between readers, and strengthen the library's role as a leader within your community—and its multiple sub-communities.

# Purpose in My Pocket:
# A Book Club Focused on Special Education

**CAPITAL REGION BOARD OF COOPERATIVE EDUCATIONAL SERVICES**

**ALBANY, NEW YORK**

**COMMUNITY TYPE: SUBURBAN**

Working with special education students can be full of extremes—from extraordinarily gratifying to highly stressful, with long hours and mountains of paperwork that extend well beyond the classroom. Burnout is a real concern. So the Capital Region Board of Cooperative Educational Services (BOCES), a nonprofit governmental agency that provides shared special education services for 174 New York school districts, created a book club to help special education teachers connect and get reinvigorated.

"In this era of ever-changing expectations in education, it can be difficult to remember why you chose the profession you did, and to make time for yourself," says special ed teacher Marissa Skinner, the club's creator. "We read books that make you remember why you got into teaching."

Once a month, special ed teachers—and the occasional parent, librarian, or speech therapist—make their way from across the BOCES service area to the agency's headquarters in Albany. The members read fiction and memoirs written by people with special needs, or accounts by their parents, teachers, or loved ones. To add to the learning, Skinner uses TED Talks and YouTube videos to further illustrate some topics raised in the books. Members can get professional development credits for attending the group.

Successful book titles tell in detail what it is like to live with and raise children with alternate needs—the "gritty truth," Skinner says. Favorites have included *The Reason I Jump: The Inner Voice of a Thirteen-Year-Old Boy with Autism* by Naoki Higashida, a memoir that invites readers into how an autistic mind thinks, feels, perceives, and responds; *Following Ezra: What One Father Learned about Gumby, Otters, Autism, and Love from His Extraordinary Son* by Tom Fields-Meyer, the story of a father and son on their journey of the boy's diagnosis; and *Kissing Doorknobs* by Terry Spencer Hesser, a young adult novel about a teen diagnosed with obsessive compulsive disorder.

"We've had many moments of laughter and tears," Skinner says. "A lot of emotion comes out as readers connect to moments in the text that remind them of students they have worked with or their own children."

Since Capital Region BOCES teachers work over a huge geographic area—one-third of the state—some teachers must travel long distances to attend the 4:00 p.m. Tuesday meetings. Still, the club's popularity has soared; membership has grown from 10 to nearly 40 members since the group formed in late 2017.

"We have people who drive forty-five minutes from their home school district every month. We have people who come in blizzards," Skinner says. "When I announced that we would be taking two months off last summer, there was practically rioting."

## Nurse Book Club

**INDIANAPOLIS PUBLIC LIBRARY, EAST 38TH STREET BRANCH**
**INDIANAPOLIS, INDIANA**
COMMUNITY TYPE: URBAN

The Nurse Book Club got its start when librarian Shanika Heyward was approached by an administrator at Avondale Meadows HealthNet, a nonprofit corporation that provides primary care health services to the medically underserved. HealthNet's medical staff are spread over eight centers, seven school-based clinics, and other locations throughout Indianapolis's low-income neighborhoods.

"Nurses and doctors spend a lot of time helping other people get well, but they tend to neglect their own health," Heyward says. "We thought a book club could be a way to let the staff connect with one another, talk about life-work balance, and build a stronger work community."

The monthly book club meetings took place in the evenings at one of HealthNet's clinics. Unlike a typical book club that reads one book per meeting, each session covered a single chapter of *Patients Come Second: Leading Change by Changing the Way You Lead*. In the book, author Paul Spiegelman argues that in order to successfully treat and retain patients, health care institutions need to adopt a philosophy where health care workers are valued, nurtured, and connected to a higher purpose. Attendance at the club was consistently high, and participants were engaged. "I barely had to facilitate," Heyward says. "They empowered themselves."

"It has been very rewarding to see their mindset," she says. "They reminded me a lot of librarians—both professions are so passionate about public service, although the services we provide are so different. It was a learning experience for me as well."

The Nurse Book Club was designed to sunset after reading *Patients Come Second*, but HealthNet has approached the library about offering the book club again. The books also had a second life: when the club ended, the library gifted the books to members, asking them to give the book away to another colleague.

## Cool Kids Book Group

**TROY PUBLIC LIBRARY | TROY, MICHIGAN**

**COMMUNITY TYPE: SUBURBAN**

Recent studies have shown that a person's relationships at work can impact his or her overall health and well-being. Plus, most of us *have* to work—why not make it more enjoyable?

Created by the Troy Public Library, the Cool Kids Book Group is a club for employees of the city of Troy, Michigan. The group comprises workers from across city departments, including public works, purchasing, the city attorney's office, planning, economic development, and of course, the public library.

The inspiration for a city employee book group came from a long-standing weekly meeting of city department heads. After those meetings, colleagues from various departments would approach library director Cathleen Russ for book recommendations. Those books, Russ learned, would then be passed from person to person around city hall. "I would loan out my copy of a book, and it would come back to me six months later, and four employees had read it," she recalls.

One day, a group of department heads was having a post-meeting chat about their current reads. "Someone walked by and said, 'What are the cool kids reading this time?'" Russ recalls. "It struck me that instead of having a harried talk after a meeting, we should have a book club." (That offhand comment also inspired the club's name.)

Once a month since then, a group of 10 to 15 city employees—not just department heads, but workers at all levels—have gathered in the library for a lunchtime book chat on Friday afternoons. (The library is located right next door to city hall, where most city employees work.) The club enjoys an eclectic mix of titles; favorites have included *Born a Crime*, the memoir of Trevor Noah; *It's Kind of a Funny Story*, a young adult novel by Ned Vizzini; and *The Sisters Brothers*, a Western by Patrick DeWitt. Whatever the title, Russ says the staffers' diverse knowledge and experience make for thought-provoking conversation.

"[It's interesting] to read *Radium Girls* with our city attorney, or to get the insights of my coworkers who know about city planning or repairing water mains," Russ says. "It's fascinating what they bring to the discussion. You go, 'Wow. Those are 200 things I have never thought of before.'"

The Cool Kids Book Group has also had an impact on work relationships. While Troy city employees have always gotten along well, the book club has fostered a new understanding and respect for one another's roles, Russ says. Best of all, members have gotten to know one another better. "We went from being a disparate group of city employees to being a book club, a group of people who enjoy each other's company and appreciate the stimulating discussions," she says. "Instead of calling MaryBeth, the purchasing director, now I'm calling MaryBeth, my friend."

## Faculty YA Book Club

**NORTH LITTLE ROCK HIGH SCHOOL LIBRARY**

**NORTH LITTLE ROCK, ARKANSAS**

COMMUNITY TYPE: SUBURBAN

If you want to get your students to read more, you could create a book club for the students. Or you could do what North Little Rock High School Library did: create a book club for the teachers.

"We have 2,500 students in our school and no time in the schedule for student book clubs. Most of our students ride the bus, so they don't have transportation," says media specialist Macy Purtle. "We have found that getting teachers excited about YA lit is an effective way to get students excited about YA lit."

Their solution was the Faculty YA Book Club. Once a month, between 6 and 15 teachers would meet after school at a local restaurant or at a teacher's home for a discussion of a young adult book. The goal was for faculty members to learn more about YA fiction so they could recommend books to their students.

"I've found that students want to read what their teachers are reading," Purtle says. "If a teacher reads a passage from a novel in class to show an example of theme or style, many students want to check out that book. This book club is just a way of trying to make that happen more often."

Memorable titles have included *Between Shades of Gray* by Ruta Sepetys, an account of a fifteen-year-old Lithuanian girl's relocation to a Siberian work camp in the wake of the Soviet Union's invasion of her country in 1940; *Ready Player One* by Ernest Cline, the dystopian science fiction novel-turned-major motion picture; and *The Hate U Give* by Angie Thomas, the story of a sixteen-year-old African American girl who witnesses the police shooting of a childhood friend. *The Hate U Give* was an especially poignant and emotional read after a North Little Rock High School student was killed in a traffic stop with police, Purtle says.

Scheduling has proven to be a challenge, so for the 2018–19 school year the book club transitioned to a Google Classroom, which contains book synopses, trailers, and interviews with the authors.

## Arizona Opera Book Club

**ARIZONA OPERA | PHOENIX AND TUCSON, ARIZONA**

**COMMUNITY TYPE: URBAN**

Since 1971, the Arizona Opera (formerly the Tucson Opera Company) has produced fully staged operas, concerts, and programs throughout the state of Arizona. In 2015, the company found a new way to engage opera enthusiasts: an Opera Book Club.

The Arizona Opera Book Club meets about five times per year—once for each production in the season—in both Phoenix and Tucson, where the company performs. Book selections are chosen to complement the current production. For example, when the Arizona Opera performed *María de Buenos Aires*, a tango opera with music by Astor Piazzolla, the book club read the novel *The Gods of Tango* by Carolina de Robertis. Adding another interesting element, the discussion was led by a champion tango-dancing duo.

"It was particularly engaging because the dancers could give insight into tango and fill in the gaps, giving historical and cultural context that might be hard to come by for the average person," says Kyle Homewood, Arizona Opera's director of community engagement and special programs.

The Opera Book Club appeals to two types of attendees, Homewood says: regular opera patrons who are looking to add another dimension to their opera experience, and people who are not yet familiar with opera, but are drawn to the book club structure. "Many people hear about us online or through friends or social media, and through the book club they find a relationship with the operatic art form," he says.

The Arizona Opera partners with a local independent bookstore for its Phoenix book club meetings; members can enjoy a drink from the store's café and can purchase their books on-site. This helps both the opera company and the bookstore reach a new audience and "amplifies our message," Homewood says. In Tucson, where the group tends to be smaller, the book club meets in a local gallery space.

Opera lovers may be a niche audience, but engaging people with shared passions can pay off in the form of a strong, enthusiastic group. "When fans can get together and delve deeper, they're a more reliable audience base and they're more invested," Homewood says.

# GET QUIRKY

**D**o you ever feel like your book club is just too . . . normal? Maybe you're struggling to differentiate your club from dozens of other reading groups in your region, or perhaps you've just fallen into the all-too-familiar rut of "read-talk-repeat."

Whatever your situation, the following book clubs may serve as inspiration. They have carved a niche for themselves with creative activities; found ways to mix up their reading lists; engaged members' dark and even morbid thoughts; and learned that silence can truly be a blessing.

# Book to Art Club (aka The B2A Club)

**CAMAS PUBLIC LIBRARY | CAMAS, WASHINGTON**
**COMMUNITY TYPE: SUBURBAN**

The club's tagline is "Read, Make, Talk"—but it's the "make" that tends to pique people's interest. At first, B2A seems like a typical book club: everyone reads the same book and comes ready to talk about it. But in addition to their reading assignment, members also create a piece of artwork at home and bring it to the meeting to share.

Book club leader Judy Wile learned about the Book to Art Club model through the now-shuttered Library as Incubator Project, and she was intrigued. Libraries across the country had created an informal network of clubs that merged reading with art. As a longtime leader of craft programs—and a lover of book clubs—Wile was hooked. "I thought, 'Oh God, this is tailor-made for me,'" she said.

The group meets every other month in a comfortable meeting room at the Camas Public Library. (Given the added time commitment of creating a piece of art, Wile found that monthly meetings were too demanding.) After discussing the book, members do a show-and-tell of their artwork, explaining their choices and the materials they used.

They use a loose definition of "art"; everything is welcome, from traditional drawing and painting to performances to culinary creations. When the club read *True Grit* by Charles Portis, one reader brought sugar cookies decorated with scenes from the book; others came decked out in cowboy hats and duster coats or brought handmade wreaths decorated with tiny whiskey bottles. Wile made s'mores for the group to snack on.

Regardless of artistic ability, Wile says, it's fun for readers to flex an often-unused creative muscle. "When you're reading a book and you know you need to make an art project, you read it a little differently," she said. "It takes it a step further."

## Boneyard Bookworms

**LAUREL HILL AND WEST LAUREL HILL CEMETERIES**

**PHILADELPHIA AND BALA CYNWYD, PENNSYLVANIA**

COMMUNITY TYPE: URBAN AND SUBURBAN

Located in Philadelphia's East Falls neighborhood, Laurel Hill Cemetery sits on seventy-eight picturesque acres overlooking the Schuylkill River. Founded in 1836 by the librarian and editor John Jay Smith and three other businessmen, the cemetery is home to more than 33,000 monuments and holds a unique designation as a National Historic Landmark.

Another thing that makes Laurel Hill Cemetery unique is that it has its own book club. Since 2011, the Boneyard Bookworms have met monthly on Thursday evenings, alternating between the Philadelphia graveyard and its sister cemetery, West Laurel Hill, in suburban Bala Cynwyd. Meetings take place inside the cemeteries' historic buildings or funeral home. To keep the conversation fresh, each discussion is led by a different club member or representative of one of the cemeteries.

And what does a cemetery book club read? "We tend to read more death-related books than an average club," says Rachel Wolgemuth, the cemeteries' administrator. Favorites have included *Destiny of the Republic: A Tale of Madness, Medicine and the Murder of a President* by Candice Millard, a telling of James Garfield's rise to the presidency and eventual assassination; and *The Immortal Life of Henrietta Lacks* by Rebecca Skloot, about a poor African American woman whose cancer cells were harvested for scientific research without her consent.

Hosting a book club in a cemetery has some advantages; for example, before a discussion about *Close to Shore: The Terrifying Shark Attacks of 1916* by Michael Capuzzo, the group drove through the cemetery to the burial site of the shark attack victim, Charles Vansant, whose death may have served as inspiration for the movie *Jaws*. When the group has read other books with ties to people interred in the cemeteries, Wolgemuth brings along portraits of the individuals or shares tidbits from their lives. "People really like that," she says. "It connects the books to where they are."

Meeting in a cemetery also requires a degree of sensitivity—especially at West Laurel Hill, which is still actively burying people. (Laurel Hill is mainly historic.) But Wolgemuth says Boneyard Bookworms is a powerful way to get the community more comfortable with the cemeteries. "We use our events and book club to bring people through our gates and get them to see who we are," she says. "Cemeteries are as much for the living as they are for the dead. Once we explain our mission, people get it."

## Silent Reading Book Club

**SKAGWAY PUBLIC LIBRARY | SKAGWAY, ALASKA**

**COMMUNITY TYPE: RURAL**

"Reading allowed, not aloud," say the signs for the Skagway Public Library's Silent Reading Book Club.

The club's premise is simple: members congregate in a public space—generally a hotel lobby or local distillery—to read quietly to themselves.

There is no pressure to share and no assigned reading; participants bring whatever book has been on their nightstands. At the end of the hour, members sometimes chat with one another and swap book recommendations—but only if they feel like it.

An introvert's dream, silent book clubs are popping up in libraries, bars, and coffee shops across the country. Many are affiliated with Silent Book Club, an international network of silent reading clubs (visit silentbook.club for a list of chapters); others, like Skagway's club, are homegrown efforts with a few people enjoying some quiet reading time together.

The library director, Julene Brown, had taken note of the silent reading club trend online and was intrigued by the idea. Then, in spring 2018, she attended a talk by the travel writer Pico Iyer, author of *The Art of Stillness: Adventures in Going Nowhere*, at a Skagway writers symposium. After reading some of Iyer's work about the benefits of slowing down and being still, Brown was inspired to bring more stillness to her library. She started by offering silent hours in the library's conference room, and then expanded to the Silent Reading Book Club.

"People don't have to worry about completing their reading, they don't feel like they're doing homework," says Brown. "I wanted to encourage people to set time aside to just sit and read."

## Talk Dewey to Me

**JEFF DAVIS COUNTY LIBRARY | FORT DAVIS, TEXAS**
COMMUNITY TYPE: RURAL

There's nothing like pushing readers out of their comfort zones to keep a discussion fresh. The Talk Dewey to Me book club takes members on a walk through the Dewey Decimal System, from the 000s (General References or Works) through the 900s (History and Biography). Participants read one book per month, in order, from each of the ten subject categories; they round out the year with autobiographies and memoirs. The titles are generally nonfiction, though there is an opportunity to delve into literature in the 800s.

In this remote region in the high mountain desert, Talk Dewey to Me attracts a mostly female crowd who are interested in reading something besides fiction—which the numerous other book clubs in town have covered. "The book club was suggested by a library patron, and it's the only book club the library has offered," says library director Gwin Grimes. "All the other book clubs in the tri-county area are private, and meetings are held in members' homes, so this is the only 'open to the public' book club."

One stand-out title for this group was *Quiet: The Power of Introverts in a World That Can't Stop Talking* by Susan Cain (155.232, Differential & Developmental Psychology – Individual Psychology). "We had both introverts and extroverts in the discussion, and the book really affected the members and helped them to understand others—sometimes others in their own families," Grimes says.

## Donuts & Death

**SPRINGFIELD-GREENE COUNTY LIBRARY | SPRINGFIELD, MISSOURI**
COMMUNITY TYPE: URBAN

Horror books and fried confections may not seem to be an obvious pairing. But Konrad Stump makes it work. "We indulge our fears while indulging our sweet tooth," says Stump, the local history associate at the Springfield-Greene County Library and creator of the Donuts & Death book club.

Stump started Donuts & Death in 2015 to appeal to horror fiction readers, a population that he says was going unserved. "I have always been a horror fan, from the days of *Goosebumps*, *Are You Afraid of the Dark?* and the permanently scarring story *The Green Ribbon*," he says. "I didn't see a lot geared toward horror fans in my district, and I knew I couldn't be the only fan out there."

For a meeting spot, he decided on Hurts Donut, a popular doughnut shop, close to Missouri State University in downtown Springfield, which he thought would appeal to young people. "I'm a firm believer that emerging adults don't want to go to a library meeting room to discuss books with strangers," Stump says. "Take your idea out into the community, preferably to a place with food."

Donuts & Death meets at 6:00 p.m. on Tuesdays; members slide into a large booth at the doughnut shop, and if needed, they pull up extra chairs. Each gathering begins with Stump raffling off a vintage horror paperback (he picks them up for a dollar or two at a local book shop) and handing out a short story for members to take home for later.

Then it's on to the horror. Successful titles have included *Gilded Needles* by Michael McDowell, a revenge story set in 1880s New York; *Elizabeth* by Ken Greenhall, told from the point of view of a fourteen-year-old sociopath; and *The Godsend* by Bernard Taylor, about a family that takes in a seemingly sweet but murderous child. "Choosing titles where there is conflict, where some people will like the characters and some will hate them, helps facilitate discussion," Stump says. "If everyone thinks everything is just dandy, then there's really nothing to talk about."

Stump's library gives him plenty of creative freedom, so he doesn't have to censor his book choices. But some things are definitely off-limits, he has learned. "I have to take into account what doesn't appeal to my group," he says. "They do not want to read about gore or violence toward women, and I better not choose a book where a dog dies."

## WHERE ARE ALL THE MEN?

There's no denying it: book clubs are dominated by women. This is not new, incidentally; book clubs date back to at least the 1630s, when the Puritan Anne Hutchinson organized a female discussion group to study the Bible in her colonial Massachusetts home. But sometimes it's nice to have some gender diversity—whether your goal is to bring new viewpoints into the room, or to offer programming that fills a gap in your current outreach.

It might sound obvious, but if you want more men to show up, you're going to have to promote the group to men. If you have other library programs with a largely male audience, start by making an appearance there. Consider creating a postcard (with a gender-neutral design) and sharing it with organizations and service clubs in your region. You may also wish to recruit a male volunteer to facilitate the group; he may be willing to bring some friends.

Next, choose books that are more appealing to men. We all know that reading tastes vary widely, but we'll have to generalize here. Steer away from "women's fiction" and toward memoirs or nonfiction books about sports, history, pop culture, or business. Also keep your eyes open for fiction that has broad appeal. Some of our favorite novels in this regard: *Revolutionary Road* by Richard Yates, *Shotgun Lovesongs* by Nickolas Butler, *The Yellow Birds* by Kevin Powers, *The Unlikely Pilgrimage of Harold Fry* by Rachel Joyce, and *Salt to the Sea* by Ruta Sepetys.

A final word of advice: as you are making changes, be sure to pause and get feedback from male coworkers, board members, or other men in your life. ❀

# Books & Bars

**FRIENDS OF ST. PAUL LIBRARY, LOFT LITERARY CENTER, SUBTEXT BOOKS,
MOON PALACE BOOKS | ST. PAUL AND MINNEAPOLIS, MINNESOTA**
**COMMUNITY TYPE: URBAN**

Books & Bars' tagline is "reinventing the book club," and with good reason. If you wandered into one of the club's monthly gatherings—held in two locations in the Twin Cities, a Minneapolis brewery and a St. Paul café—what you saw wouldn't look like a typical reading group. Part book club, part interactive performance, the meetings feature moderator Jeff Kamin working the room with a wireless microphone, running Phil Donahue–style from table to table to invite attendees to share their opinions, and injecting comedic banter honed from his days as an improv comic.

Known as the largest book club in the Twin Cities area, Books & Bars generally attracts an audience of seventy-five or more—largely people in their twenties and thirties, and a good mix of women and men. All of this was part of Kamin's unique vision when he created the club in 2004.

"I had moved to St. Paul from Los Angeles and wanted to be in a book club, but all the book clubs I knew were entirely female, and they literally wouldn't let me join. They said, 'You wouldn't like it. We talk about the book for fifteen minutes and then we drink wine,'" he recalls. "I said, I want a book club where anyone can go, it's open to the public, it's free, people can get a drink, and guys feel as comfortable there as women." Books & Bars got its start at a bookstore where Kamin was employed; when the shop closed down, he decided to take on the project himself.

A self-described book lover, Kamin chooses Books & Bars' titles, but he invites attendees to vote for their favorites at events and via social media. "I look at what's going on in the world when I pick our book selections," he says. Reads have included *The Handmaid's Tale* by Margaret Atwood, *Ready Player One* by Ernest Cline, and *Kafka on the Shore* by Haruki Murakami. The discussions are frequently paired with author visits, either in person or via Skype; notable visitors have included Cheryl Strayed, Susan Orlean, and Amor Towles.

One of Kamin's favorite things about Book & Bars is the diversity of opinions in the room. "When you have an age range of 21 to 71, the 21-year-olds take is very different than the 71-year-old's," he says. "But we're all on an equal footing. You might be an English major, but your opinion is no different than the plumber sitting next to you."

# Steamy Reads Book Club

**WELLS BRANCH COMMUNITY LIBRARY | AUSTIN, TEXAS**

COMMUNITY TYPE: SUBURBAN

Why should romance and erotica readers feel the need to keep their reading habits under wraps? Since 2013, the Wells Branch Community Library has celebrated, not shunned, the erotic fiction genre with the Steamy Reads Book Club.

The club, which appeals to women in the thirty-to-sixty age range, meets monthly on Wednesday evenings in the library's Quiet Reading Room. Of course, it's not quiet for long; meetings tend to get raucous. "A discussion of euphemisms and tropes is always a good way to get people talking—there's usually a lot of giggling involved!" says Brittany Patrick, the adult program and service librarian. The library also provides hot (i.e., steamy) drinks like tea or hot chocolate and sweets to make the gathering more social.

"Our members like their books 'extra steamy' and often select off-the-wall plots simply for the fun of it," says Patrick. Favorites have included *Enchanted: Erotic Bedtime Stories for Women* by Nancy Madore, a collection of erotic stories that members enjoyed for its positive depictions of women; and *How to Flirt with a Naked Werewolf* by Molly Harper, which appealed to fans of paranormal romance, especially "shifting," in which humans turn into animals. ("The subgenre is more popular than I expected it to be," Patrick notes.) *Fifty Shades of Grey* by E. L. James was a mainstream pick that caused a surge in attendance.

There are a few considerations to keep in mind when planning an erotic fiction book club, Patrick says. It can be difficult to attract new members, especially when regular group members veer toward niche subgenres. "Since our club tends toward very steamy novels—hence the name—those who are interested in soft romance generally don't attend for very long," she says. And unlike other book clubs, the covers of the selected books can pose a marketing problem; on occasion, the library has kept book covers off its marketing materials because of the amount of skin showing or suggestive poses.

But overall, the club is lots of fun for everyone, Patrick says. "It's fun to be able to talk about even the steamiest of books without worrying about embarrassment or judgment," she says. "Even if members hated that month's book, it's always a good time discussing why—often it's because of bad writing, and that just becomes fun to laugh about in its own right."

# Pre-Pub Book Club

**COMMERCE TOWNSHIP COMMUNITY LIBRARY | COMMERCE TOWNSHIP, MICHIGAN**
**COMMUNITY TYPE: SUBURBAN**

As a librarian and book reviewer, Marika Zemke received boxes of advance reader copies for soon-to-be-published fiction and nonfiction. She was never quite sure what to do with them all—publisher rules prohibited them from being sold, and there were too many to add to her own collection—until she came up with an idea: a book club where members read pre-publication books and learn about the publishing industry in the process. Plus, they'd get to keep the books.

"I researched and couldn't find any other book clubs that read advance copies, so I thought, I'm going to start my own," says Zemke, the adult services manager of the Commerce Township Community Library. "People loved it."

The Pre-Pub Book Club started meeting on Monday evenings in 2009. Since Zemke usually only had one copy of any given book, the members couldn't read the same titles. Instead, she would select a handful of upcoming titles to discuss at each meeting. In a brief presentation, she would cover the book's synopsis, its cover, genre, author, publisher, and even information about its marketing plan. (Publishers often share information about pre-publication marketing plans, including PR appearances, along with the advance reader copies.)

"We would look at the whole package—the feel of the book, the kind of paper it's printed on. Sometimes a book would come wrapped as a gift, or in a box with cookies and candy. This tells me the publisher is spending a lot on marketing, and they think it's going to be a big seller," Zemke says. "Our members found it fascinating. They crave the behind-the-scenes stuff."

After sharing the week's books, members could select one to take home; often they would arrange to swap books so several people could read them. The next month, readers would start by discussing what they had read the month before.

After about five years, attendance in the Pre-Pub Book Club started to wane, and members suggested moving the meetings to the daytime. Zemke decided to combine the Pre-Pub Book Club with an existing Monday morning library book club. For the first fifteen minutes, the group talks about and distributes the advance reader copies, and then the group transitions to talking about that month's read.

"They love it because it's one less trip to the library," Zemke says. "And I still get to talk about the books and hype them up. It's fun, and it's promoting books and authors. I call myself a book pimp."

# CHAPTER EIGHT

# ENCOURAGE ACTIVISM

**O**ne thing is for certain: we are living through exciting times, political and socially. Regardless of where on the political spectrum your community lies, the things happening outside your library's walls provide extremely engaging discussion topics for book clubs. And you don't need to stop at just talking; a book club can serve as a jumping-off point for activism.

Of course, activism means different things to different people. The following book clubs introduce patrons to politics and art they may find controversial; inspire teens to take action on social justice topics (or just make their school community a little kinder); and bring pressing national issues into focus on a local level.

# R.A.D.A. (Read. Awareness. Dialogue. Action.)

### DENVER PUBLIC LIBRARY | DENVER, COLORADO
### COMMUNITY TYPE: URBAN

The Denver Public Library's R.A.D.A (Read. Awareness. Dialogue. Action.) series provides a safe space to discuss some of the issues and movements of the day with respect and compassion. Its first meeting took place in 2015—a difficult time, recalls the adult services librarian James Allen Davis, when residents were struggling with the tragic deaths of African Americans like Trayvon Martin, Michael Brown, and Sandra Bland. "People would come into the library and say, 'Oh my goodness, did you see what just happened to this young black kid?'" Davis says. "We thought, our library has to be more relevant. What can we do to provide a place where people can have an open discussion and process what is happening in their communities?"

The group started with pilot discussions at two library branches. The programs focused on popular nonfiction titles: *The New Jim Crow: Mass Incarceration in the Age of Colorblindness* by Michelle Alexander, and *The Griots of Oakland: Voices from the African American Oral History Project* by Angela Zusman. A facilitator—a member of the library staff committee that runs R.A.D.A.—helped guide the discussions, and a strategic illustrator volunteered to record the conversations in graphic form. At the back of the room, a resource table, curated by the R.A.D.A. committee, shared information about organizations where people could get involved.

Setting ground rules was important to keeping the conversation respectful. "We remind everyone to act like adults and to focus on the topic and not the person speaking," says librarian Hadiya Evans. "These are sensitive topics, but we still have to be mindful of one another."

Since 2015, the Denver Public Library has held thirteen R.A.D.A. conversations in nine library branches—typically three per year, spread over the spring and fall. Topics have included immigration (*Americanah* by Chimamanda Ngozi Adichie), gentrification (*How to Kill a City: Gentrification, Inequality, and the Fight for the Neighborhood* by Peter Moskowitz), and racism and the legacy of oppression (*White Rage: The Unspoken Truth of Our Racial Divide* by Carol Anderson). Attendees are invited whether or not they have read the book, and attendance generally ranges from 15 to 30 people (although a special event about police violence featuring Jason Reynolds, author of *All American Boys*, attracted more than 100).

R.A.D.A. has impacted how the library listens to the community, Evans says. "In our conversation about *White Rage*, a few people said they weren't sure how to respond when they are bystanders to people experiencing racism or micro-aggressions," she says. "So we created a workshop, with scenarios, to help give them those tools. We're listening, and we're continuing to be responsive."

## IDEA Book Club
## (Inclusion, Diversity, Equity, and Accessibility)

**CRYSTAL BRIDGES MUSEUM OF AMERICAN ART LIBRARY**

**BENTONVILLE, ARKANSAS**

COMMUNITY TYPE: URBAN, SURROUNDED BY RURAL

The Crystal Bridges Museum of American Art was founded in 2005 with a unique mission: to bring American art and art history to the masses, specifically the low-income communities around Bentonville, Arkansas, which otherwise might not have much exposure to the arts. The museum does not shy away from bold exhibitions; in early 2018, it became the first museum in the nation to show the Tate Modern's "Soul of a Nation: Art in the Age of Black Power."

In a region that lacks diversity and educational opportunities, the exhibition raised some eyebrows. Jeanne Besaw, the museum's head of library services, thought Crystal Bridges' book club—which, until then, read conventional best-sellers—could help offer some much-needed context for the art. "What if our focus was to help inform our public, as well as our staff and volunteers, about what's coming next at the museum?" she says. The response surprised even Besaw. "It was huge. The book club swelled from 4 people to 22 people, practically overnight."

The IDEA Book Club's first read was *The Underground Railroad* by Colson Whitehead. The novel—which tells the story of two slaves escaping from their Georgia plantation—was "explosive" for some readers. "I had a woman throw a book at me. She was in her eighties, and she had been informed her entire life, even in school, that slaves chose slavery. . . . She was deeply offended by it," Besaw says. But a few weeks later, the woman came back. "She apologized, and she had been actively learning more. It was difficult for her to wrap her mind around the fact that she had been misinformed."

Since then, the IDEA Book Club has read *When They Call You a Terrorist: A Black Lives Matter Memoir* by Asha Bandele and Patrisse Cullors, and *Killers of the Flower Moon: The Osage Murders and the Birth of the FBI* by David Grann. They have also experimented with comparing two titles: half the group read James Baldwin's 1963 essay collection, *The Fire Next Time*, and half read Jessmyn Ward's 2016 response, *The Fire This Time: A New Generation Speaks about Race*.

The club now offers three meetings: one for the general public and two for staff. "We're doing something different," Besaw says. "Just getting to do these things and ask these questions has been remarkable."

## Understanding Differences: Expanding Our Social Awareness Book Club

### JONES LIBRARY | AMHERST, MASSACHUSETTS

#### COMMUNITY TYPE: SUBURBAN

Located in the Pioneer Valley in western Massachusetts, the town of Amherst is home to three colleges and universities, a bustling cultural scene, and an educated, largely liberal population. Living there, says Jones Library volunteer Caryl-Rose Pofcher, it's easy to find yourself in a bubble where most of the people around you share your beliefs.

"We almost have a greater need to be reminded of the world outside Happy Valley," says Pofcher, using residents' nickname for the region.

The Understanding Differences Book Club invites adults to read books that encourage them to think outside familiar boxes. "It's the old 'walk a mile in someone else's shoes' concept," Pofcher says. "It isn't a political activist group, it isn't fighting social injustice. It's really trying to broaden our perspectives."

Each gathering starts the same way: members take turns sharing brief (two or three minutes' worth) thoughts or impressions about the book. No one may ask a question or start a discussion until everyone who wishes to speak has done so. This gives the quieter members a chance to be heard. "By the time we've gone around the room, people are eager to start commenting and asking each other questions," Pofcher says. The conversation evolves from there.

Successful titles give insight into the daily reality of people who don't often break into the mainstream; these have included *An Indigenous People's History of the United States* by Roxanne Dunbar-Ortiz, *The New Jim Crow: Mass Incarceration in the Age of Colorblindness* by Michelle Alexander, and *Look Me in the Eye: My Life with Asperger's* by John Elder Robison. Books that are too depressing aren't as well received, Pofcher says. "If we read two or three such books in a row, we imperil the existence of the group," she says. "Books don't have to be feel-good and rarely are entirely. Finding a balance is what mostly works for us."

## Books for a Better World

### RICHMOND PUBLIC LIBRARY | RICHMOND, VIRGINIA
#### COMMUNITY TYPE: URBAN

Books for a Better World is a monthly author series and book club that focuses on themes of social justice, history, healing, and memory. Each month, participants read a book by a different local author, and then the author visits the library's Hull Street Branch for a book talk and Q&A.

With several colleges and universities in Richmond—including Virginia State University, Randolph Macon College, and the University of Richmond—the library has a rich academic community to tap as potential speakers. "I select authors who are accustomed to engaging groups. Most are college professors," says Natalie Draper, the branch's library/community services manager.

Draper doesn't shy away from unconventional reads, which keeps the book list varied. "Don't fear nonfiction, controversial topics, academic titles, or books from 'vanity' presses," she says. "Get out and connect with your local author and academic community." To start, she recommends connecting with nearby colleges and universities, small presses, and historical societies.

One standout discussion at Books for a Better World was about *Writing Our Way Out: Memoirs from Jail*. The book's author, David Coogan, a Virginia Commonwealth University professor who teaches writing workshops at the Richmond City Jail, invited three men whose stories were featured in the book. The conversation lasted past the library's closing time. After the program, a regular patron approached Draper to say thanks. "He frequents the library for the things everyone does—entertainment, technology, friendly conversation—but he misses the book club because that's the time when he meets with his [parole officer]," Draper says. "I had no idea. He made special arrangements that night so he wouldn't miss it."

Most of Draper's book selections lean toward the left on the political spectrum, which she says matches the values of her community. But being accused of partisan politics is a concern. "I will not shy away from tough social issues, but if you are selecting books on themes like these, you should be prepared to defend the selections," she says.

## Fearless Readers

**ELIZABETH PUBLIC LIBRARY | ELIZABETH, NEW JERSEY**

**COMMUNITY TYPE: URBAN**

Fearless Readers is a book club designed and led by teenagers (ages 12 to 19)—some who attend high school in Elizabeth, New Jersey, just outside Newark, and others who have dropped out. All of the club's themes and titles are discussed with a lens on social justice and social change; whenever possible, guest speakers and activities help members explore how they can turn ideas into action.

The key to Fearless Readers' success has been giving agency to its members, says teen librarian Tracy Robinson. The teens are empowered to choose the themes, titles, discussion questions, and activities. "Trust your teens," Robinson says. "The more power they are given, the more ownership they will feel over the project, and the result will absolutely be a stronger club."

Popular titles have included *The Hate U Give* by Angie Thomas, *Shadowshaper* by Daniel José Older, and *Queer: A Graphic History* by Meg-John Barker. For *Queer: A Graphic History*, a speaker from Garden State Equality met with a group of nearly thirty LGBTQIA+ teens for a discussion about their rights and how to safely assert them. During the presentation, a transgender student shared that he avoided using the restroom at school for fear of being forced to use the girls' restroom, and he said that most of his teachers refuse to use his preferred name and pronouns.

"[The speaker] responded by saying that it is every New Jersey student's right to be called by whatever names and pronouns make them feel comfortable, and that the school does not even need to share these choices with parents," Robinson says. "The student was stunned." As a result of that discussion, a county legislator called a meeting with the Board of Education to discuss gender-neutral bathrooms, and the students have since taken steps to start Elizabeth's first-ever Gay Straight Alliance.

When tackling weighty topics such as this, discussions can become heated. Robinson has found that pointing to the text is the best thing to do in those moments. "Do not fear conflict," she says. "If members don't see eye to eye, it is a gift—a perfect opportunity to explore the disparities that are reflected in our society, on a large scale."

"Ultimately, for us, the most important thing is making sure that all of our members feel empowered to lead discussions and take actions that work toward social change," Robinson says. "This feeling of empowerment keeps members coming back."

Fearless Readers was born out of the Great Stories Club, a grant program of the American Library Association that provides training and resources to assist library professionals in leading reading and discussion groups with underserved youth. You can learn more about the Great Stories Club in the "Resources" section at the end of this book.

## Get Some Kindness

**HACKETT HIGH SCHOOL LIBRARY | HACKETT, ARKANSAS**
COMMUNITY TYPE: RURAL

Everyone could benefit from a little more kindness in their life—especially middle and high school students. In 2016, school librarian Cindy Linker and her colleague, guidance counselor Sharon Welch, decided to create a book club that focused on how kids at Hackett High School treat one another. "We didn't want to put any emphasis on bullying," Linker says. "Instead, we place great importance on acts of kindness." And so Get Some Kindness—a book club that promotes kindness activities in the school—was born.

The club's first read was *Rachel's Tears: The Spiritual Journey of Columbine Martyr Rachel Scott*, a nonfiction book about a victim of the 1999 Columbine shooting, written by the victim's parents. "Through this book, students see the impact that kindness has regardless of the consequences," Linker says. "We also look at forgiveness and how it plays such an important role in relationships and in life."

At their Thursday lunchtime meetings, Get Some Kindness members either discuss their current book (the group decides how many pages to read for the next meeting) or take part in kindness activities in collaboration with another school book club, the Leader Readers. Together, Get Some Kindness and the Leader Readers have hosted a breakfast for their teachers; placed sticky notes with handwritten inspirational messages on lockers throughout the school; made flower pins out of duct tape for cafeteria workers and left candy for bus drivers; and raised more than $600 for the Brandon Burlsworth Foundation, a Christian organization that "supports the physical and spiritual needs of children, particularly those with limited opportunities." (*Through the Eyes of a Champion: The Brandon Burlsworth Story* by Jeff Kinley was another Get Some Kindness read.)

The goal is larger than a few nice gestures, Linker says; it's fostering a culture of goodwill and respect. "We want kindness to come back around," she says. "We try to show students that it can be something that returns to people—to be a chain reaction of kindness."

## Relevant Reads

**SACRAMENTO PUBLIC LIBRARY / ROBBIE WATERS**
**POCKET-GREENHAVEN LIBRARY | SACRAMENTO, CALIFORNIA**
COMMUNITY TYPE: SUBURBAN

Based in the Pocket-Greenhaven community's library branch in southwest Sacramento, Relevant Reads is a book club that reads nonfiction books about issues that are relevant to the local community and society as a whole. Their discussions encompass the book, the issue, and steps to action.

The inspiration for Relevant Reads came from a grant-funded library program, held in 2017, in which a librarian and science expert led a conversation about the effects of climate change on the Sacramento area. "The format brought out some really great discussion," says Brendle Wells, adult materials selector for the library system. "I was also thinking that there are a lot of great books coming out right now that you really want to read, but sometimes you need motivation to read them because you know they're going to be tough."

*Evicted: Poverty and Profit in the American City* by Matthew Desmond sparked a good conversation about the housing crisis in California, which was particularly bad in the Sacramento area. *Just Mercy* by Bryan Stevenson sparked a discussion about the shooting of Stephon Clark, an unarmed African American man, by police in the backyard of his Sacramento home. *Ghosts of the Tsunami*, an account of the 2011 Japanese tsunami and its aftermath by the British reporter Richard Lloyd Parry, "worked well because of the relevance of disasters to our community (earthquakes and fires) and also because a significant portion of the community (and our book group) is Japanese American," Wells says. "We even had two practicing Buddhists in our group who were able to talk about the spiritual aspects."

Relevant Reads meetings typically end with a member asking, "What can I do now?" The answer has varied. For some books, Wells has provided information about local organizations working on a topic, or links for additional reading. Sometimes the answer is simply: spread the word. For *The Color of Law: A Forgotten History of How Our Government Segregated America* by Richard Rothstein, the group discussed how educating others is the best course of action. "You know about this now, so you can pass it on," Wells says.

# CHAPTER NINE

# MEET THEM WHERE THEY ARE

**I**f you're having trouble getting people to attend a book club at your library, consider moving your meetings to a place where people are already gathered. Getting to the library can be a barrier for many people, so it is important to try to bring library services out into the community whenever possible.

Think about where people assemble near your library. Would they be receptive to a book club? If you're not sure, visit the location and start talking with people to see if there's any interest. Working with staff at these organizations can also help you decipher what groups to target and what challenges you might face.

# Johnson Youth Center Book Club

**JUNEAU PUBLIC LIBRARY | JUNEAU, ALASKA**
COMMUNITY TYPE: RURAL

As anyone who has led a book club can attest, sometimes members really dislike a book. This occasionally happens when Andrea Hirsh, the community outreach librarian at the Juneau Public Library, leads a book club for boys aged 13 to 18 at the Johnson Youth Center, a youth detention facility. She always lets the teens know there is no shame in putting down a book that isn't enjoyable. "Reading for fun is supposed to be fun!" she says.

Because the Johnson Youth Center is a closed site, library staff don't have to worry about advertising the book club to the public. However, like other book clubs, they also face challenges with attendance, namely, that the population is always changing. The rotating nature of the facility definitely impacts book selection. "What is successful the first time might be a huge failure the next time because the participants have changed and have different interests or reading levels," Hirsh says. As a result, she has become more flexible and always has a few backup options each month in case the group's dynamics have changed.

In addition to their monthly book discussions, the book club also has phone calls with authors at least once or twice a year. After reading *Proxy*, the group called its author, Alex London. Hirsh recalls, "At one point in the call Alex said, 'I *hated* reading in high school. I don't think I ever finished a single book.'" This immediately got the boys' attention. They asked the author many questions and continued the discussion after ending the call. Hirsh remembers a boy saying, "Well, he didn't like reading and now he's a famous author! I read more now than he did, so maybe I can, too."

Other popular books have included *Winger* by Andrew Smith, *Buck: A Memoir* by MK Asante, and *The Hate U Give* by Angie Thomas. Books that address social issues the group can relate to always lead to engaging discussions. On those occasions when the boys dislike a book, Hirsh asks them to consider a few important questions, like "If you want to be an author, you should think about why you didn't like those books—what didn't work for you, and what would you change about them?"

# Cancer Center Book Club

**SANTA BARBARA PUBLIC LIBRARY | SANTA BARBARA, CALIFORNIA**
**COMMUNITY TYPE: URBAN**

Jace Turner, a community relations librarian at the Santa Barbara Public Library, had a "strong desire to take library programming out into the community—especially to those who may not otherwise be able to attend library programming at the library." As a result, the Cancer Center Book Club began meeting monthly at the Ridley-Tree Cancer Center Resource Library in February 2018.

The book club is a partnership between the Santa Barbara Public Library and the Cancer Center Resource Library, so Turner facilitates the meetings with a member of the center's staff. They try to remove barriers of participation, such as overdue fines or lost books, by allowing members to borrow a copy of the book without actually checking it out on their library account.

The book club is made up of cancer patients, caregivers, and survivors. Turner says, "The titles we choose are fiction and nonfiction, but do not relate to cancer directly—the idea is to offer a little escape from their day-to-day." Because they are aware that being sick or caring for someone who is battling an illness can be a solitary journey, the group provides a space for people to meet others who are going through the same experiences. Popular titles have included *Lab Girl* by Hope Jahren, *The Art of Hearing Heartbeats* by Jan-Philipp Sendker, and *The Power of Meaning* by Emily Esfahani Smith. All three books "kindled passionate discussions, provided opportunities to offer critical perspectives, and inspired members to relate themes in the books to their own lives, especially to their illness and outlook on life and health," notes Turner.

Like any book club, the meetings generally start with introductions, but the members also share their history with cancer, which helps to unite the group. After the book discussion, the group often continues to talk about their experiences with cancer. Turner recalls a particularly memorable conversation with a member after the discussion of *Lab Girl*. "As she was describing how much she loved the book, she broke down in tears, sharing that she was determined to finish it and had worked very hard to read the entire book—that it was the first book she's read in two years due to the side effects of the drugs she is taking for her cancer."

# Mommy Book Club

**KATY BUDGET BOOKS | HOUSTON, TEXAS**

COMMUNITY TYPE: SUBURBAN

Anna Brown, the events coordinator at Katy Budget Books, started the Mommy Book Club after becoming a mother. "I had a baby of my own and realized how little I got out anymore because I always worried about him distracting people from the purpose of gatherings," says Brown. The group is geared toward moms who would otherwise be reluctant to participate in a book club for fear of a fussy child.

Every month, the moms and their children gather at the store. Chairs are arranged in a circle, and the center is filled with toys for the kids to play with during the discussion. If members can't attend a meeting, they can still participate in the conversation on the group's Facebook page.

When it comes to book selection, Brown comments, "It seems like romance and YA titles do best for our group because they are easier to follow when you have to set them down a lot and come back to them later." Popular titles have included *Keep Her Safe* by K. A. Tucker, *Of Fire and Stars* by Audrey Coulthurst, and *The Hypnotist's Love Story* by Liane Moriarty. When the book club first started, Brown notes, "we ended up talking a lot more about our kids than the book." She took this into account for future meetings, selecting books that include parent-child relationships in order to combine personal parenting experiences with the book discussion.

Brown has a few suggestions for creating a successful book club like hers. First, it is important to be aware of a book's content, and to particularly avoid any stories that involve the death of a child. "As a new mom, I am sensitive to the fact that we're paranoid enough without reading more ways something could go wrong," Brown says.

Next, be prepared for the littlest members of the book club! Provide entertaining toys that will engage the children throughout the meeting. Finally, Brown says, "I think it definitely takes a mother of a little one to guide a group like this, because you understand how important this adult group is and how it has to function kind of chaotically in a way that I easily forgot between my eldest son and my second."

# Ferry Tales

**KITSAP REGIONAL LIBRARY | BAINBRIDGE ISLAND, WASHINGTON**
COMMUNITY TYPE: SUBURBAN

"Riding the ferry, I often saw people reading, but I didn't see those same faces in the library," says Audrey Barbakoff, the former adult services librarian at the Kitsap Regional Library. She started Ferry Tales in 2012 in hopes of bringing the library directly to people taking the commuter ferry every day from Seattle to Bainbridge Island. Although she has since vacated her position, the book club continues to meet with her replacement, John Fossett.

At first Barbakoff planned to hold a morning book club, but she says, "I learned not to interrupt people before they've had their coffee!" She didn't let this minor bump discourage her, though. Conversations with both commuters and ferry staff helped her determine what would make a book group successful with this audience. While most of the members are commuters, one older woman enjoyed a monthly ferry ride specifically for the meeting. "She would board on Bainbridge Island, ride to Seattle, stop for happy hour at a nearby restaurant, and then get back on the returning ferry to join the group," Barbakoff notes.

Despite only having about thirty minutes to meet every month, the book club has had some memorable discussions. After reading *Shiro: Wit, Wisdom, and Recipes from a Sushi Pioneer*, the author joined the group on the ferry. When they disembarked, the entire club attended a launch party at a local business. During a discussion of *The Immortal Life of Henrietta Lacks*, a member surprised the group by sharing a tube of HeLa cells from her workplace.

Part of the success of this book club is due to the library's partnership with the Washington State Ferries. They allow the library to advertise in the ferry terminals, and they remind their staff to make an announcement on meeting days. If you don't have a commuter ferry near your library, Barbakoff has other suggestions. "Look for places where people have trapped time—on the bus, in a waiting room, etc.," she says. "Where can you go to turn a tedious time into one filled with community and reading?"

## Silver Fox Audio Book Club

**BALDWINSVILLE PUBLIC LIBRARY | BALDWINSVILLE, NEW YORK**
**COMMUNITY TYPE: SUBURBAN**

Nancy Howe, a public relations and outreach librarian at the Baldwinsville Public Library, was inspired to start the Silver Fox Audio Book Club after having a conversation with the activity director at the Silver Fox Senior Center. The director was hoping to provide additional programs for the seniors at the center, and a book club run by the library seemed like a great fit. Describing the group, Howe says, "This is an audio book club for seniors, many of whom have early onset dementia, which makes reading difficult."

Each week, the group gathers at the Silver Fox Senior Center, where they start the meeting by sharing what they remember from the last week. After an hour of listening to the book together, they discuss their thoughts on the book so far. The club only listens to books that have a film adaptation, so they can watch the movie together at the library when they have finished the book. The highly anticipated movie viewings are always followed by a discussion of whether members liked the book or movie better.

Although the club prefers to read nonfiction or fiction inspired by a true story, occasionally they also select books from other genres. For someone who is experiencing memory loss, reading science fiction and fantasy novels can be particularly challenging. When listening to *The Hitchhiker's Guide to the Galaxy*, the members had a difficult time picturing what was happening at various points in the book.

*Unbroken* and *Seabiscuit* by Laura Hillenbrand and *The King's Speech* by Mark Logue and Peter Conradi have been some of the group's favorite books and have all led to fascinating discussions. Seeing the veterans in the group become emotional while listening to *Unbroken* was a particularly memorable moment. "I cried too, and we all agree that while it was difficult to listen to, we were glad we had chosen this title," Howe says.

## A NOTE ABOUT FACILITATING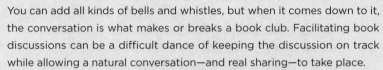

You can add all kinds of bells and whistles, but when it comes down to it, the conversation is what makes or breaks a book club. Facilitating book discussions can be a difficult dance of keeping the discussion on track while allowing a natural conversation—and real sharing—to take place.

As most seasoned book club leaders would agree, the best discussions happen when conversation is allowed to flow freely. This isn't always easy; members may not be open to sharing, especially if they don't know each other well. Preparing a list of questions will provide you with some insurance in case the conversation stalls, but with luck—and as your attendees become regulars—you may not need them.

We asked a number of book club facilitators about their strategies:

> "A lot of people disagree with the 'What did you think of the book?' opener, but it's simple, gets the conversation started, and allows you to ease into more nuanced questions."
>
> —KONRAD STUMP, Donuts & Death, Springfield-Greene County Library (book club no. 41)

> "We start off by going around the group. It encourages the quieter people to have a turn, if they want to take it. Sometimes I think having made one statement makes it easier to join in the discussion. You've broken the ice."
>
> —CARYL-ROSE POFCHER, Understanding Differences Book Club, Jones Library (book club no. 47)

> "We have five questions that we ask people to come prepared to answer—the same questions each month—including a favorite quote or moment from the book. The rest of the discussion is based on that month's book, with questions designed by me."
>
> —MARISSA SKINNER, Purpose in My Pocket, Capital Region BOCES (book club no. 32)

> "I was really nervous at first [to be facilitating a book club with people experiencing homelessness]. Do I apologize that I'm going home? Do I say nothing? The bottom line is, they didn't ask me where I was going, and I didn't ask them where they were going. We based our conversation on the present, and the present was this book and how it affected us."
>
> —JENIFER WHITMORE, Oasis Book Club, Oasis Coalition of Boston (book club no. 29)

"In Next Chapter Book Club, I start with 'Hi, how was your week?' or 'I hear someone got a gold medal in Special Olympics, can you share that?' People are bursting with news, and we try to warm people up with the social talk. Then we say, 'Okay, who wants to read first?' It's quite an honor to read first, so if someone has a birthday or got a gold medal in the Special Olympics, for example, that person gets to start, and they get to choose if we go clockwise or counterclockwise around the circle."

—PAM BROOKS, Next Chapter Book Club, Scotch Plains Public Library
(book club no. 30)

CHAPTER TEN

# SHORT ON TIME

**B**ook clubs with monthly meetings require a major time commitment from both staff and patrons. If you have people in your community who are interested in joining a book club but are unable to attend twelve meetings a year, consider modifying your meeting schedule.

Whether you make a slight adjustment to hold just nine meetings a year, or a drastic change to meet only biannually, less frequent gatherings may result in a surge in participation. Additionally, the staff may be able to procure exciting guest speakers or develop interesting activities for meetings if they are not expected to generate fresh ideas every month.

# Special Collections Book Club

## LEVI WATKINS LEARNING CENTER AT ALABAMA STATE UNIVERSITY
### MONTGOMERY, ALABAMA
#### COMMUNITY TYPE: URBAN

Once a semester, the Special Collections Book Club gathers to discuss fiction by African American authors. Members of the wider Montgomery community are encouraged to join students, faculty, and other university staff for their meetings in the Special Collections area of the Levi Watkins Learning Center at Alabama State University. Jina DuVernay, the special collections librarian, says, "My goal is to promote literacy and a safe space to meet new people, share ideas, hear new perspectives, and to essentially grow both educationally and personally."

During the first meeting of the book club, the members discussed *Silver Sparrow* by Tayari Jones. The library had received forty copies of the novel, and using the generous donation to start a book club seemed like a logical next step. The books were available for free to anyone who stopped by and asked for one. While forty copies of the book were given out, there were about twenty people in attendance at that memorable first meeting. DuVernay recalls, "It was truly gratifying to see that people were interested in reading and meeting new people and engaging in meaningful discussions."

A discussion of *The Hate U Give* by Angie Thomas drew people in for different reasons. DuVernay thinks the meeting attracted more members of the community, as well as more male students, because the book addresses police brutality and social justice. In addition to the book discussion, she created a guessing game for the meeting. Attendees were invited to predict who would be playing each character in the upcoming film adaptation for a chance to win a prize.

When it comes to starting your own book club, DuVernay says, "Use whatever you have to make it happen. Collaboration is key." Connections with the community and other departments within your organization can all be instrumental in getting your group off the ground.

# Cabin Fever Book Group

**HOWE LIBRARY | HANOVER, NEW HAMPSHIRE**
**COMMUNITY TYPE: SUBURBAN**

The Howe Library in Hanover, New Hampshire, decided to create a book club to combat the winter blues. The Cabin Fever Book Group meets just five months of the year, from November to March, and members can be found discussing both fiction and nonfiction at the library at 2:00 p.m. on the first Sunday of the month.

Megan Coleman, a public relations and outreach librarian at the Howe Library, started the Cabin Fever Book Group after hearing many people express an interest in weekend meetings. The library aims to make the book club accessible to more people by purchasing paperback copies of the book and encouraging anyone to borrow the book, even if they don't have a library card.

Popular titles have included *Cat Out of Hell* by Lynne Truss and *Master of Thieves* by Stephen Kurkjian. A discussion about *Modern Love* by Aziz Ansari also proved memorable. "Who knew when I picked this book in September that it would be so timely when we discussed this in March?" Coleman says. "I decided to go ahead despite the [sexual misconduct] allegations." In preparation for the discussion, Coleman provided everyone with a variety of articles about the Time's Up and MeToo movements, as well as the controversy surrounding the book's author. She notes, "The discussion was great, though all attendees were seniors, and I was the only person under sixty-five. I was hoping for more intergenerational viewpoints in the discussion."

During the first round of this book group, Coleman realized that interest in a program does not guarantee an audience. Even with the high circulation of book club titles, only four people participated in the most well-attended meeting. Despite the challenges, Coleman offers some encouraging advice. "Learn what you can from it—who came, who didn't, listen to any feedback you did get (good and bad), did people like your picks or not—and either tweak what you are doing or let it go." She is currently taking her own advice and contemplating how she can increase attendance at the group's next round of meetings.

# GCLD Adult Virtual Book Club

**GRAND COUNTY LIBRARY DISTRICT | GRAND COUNTY, COLORADO**

**COMMUNITY TYPE: RURAL**

Shelly Mathis, a library services specialist, and Emily Pedersen, a branch librarian, have one piece of advice for libraries: "Listen to your patrons!" When members of their community said they wanted to join a book club but did not like the demands that come with traditional groups, like required reading, Mathis and Pedersen took note. As a result, the GCLD Adult Virtual Book Club began meeting in fall 2015.

Every quarter, the group gathers at the library for a discussion fueled by food. Each meeting has a fiction and nonfiction theme like Mysteries and True Crime or Westerns and American Western History. Members are invited to choose their own books within these themes and can read as many books as they'd like throughout the quarter. During the meeting, everyone shares a summary and their thoughts on each book they read.

The loose format of the meetings provides members with new book recommendations and also leads to great conversations. As Mathis and Pedersen note, "Sometimes the stories that our club members share have everyone rolling in laughter or are extremely poignant about a serious current event. We never know what spontaneous flow the discussion will take." For those who expressed a desire to communicate more frequently, the book club has a virtual component. Members can post their thoughts and recommendations on the club's Facebook page at any time.

While the book club is open to anyone, the members are all female, ranging in age from twenty to eighty. A meeting on Culinary Lit and Cookbooks proved memorable, thanks to an eighty-year-old member of the group. Mathis and Pedersen said, "To our great delight, she brought her original edition of the first *Better Homes and Gardens* cookbook and told the tale of her adventures in Alaska trying to learn how to bake bread for her new husband and the local fishing boys in the 1950s."

# Book-Enders

**UPLAND PUBLIC LIBRARY | UPLAND, CALIFORNIA**
**COMMUNITY TYPE: SUBURBAN**

Members of the Book-Enders have been talking about books together for twenty-eight years. Every month, from October to May, the group assembles for two hours at the Upland Public Library. Their June meeting is hosted at the nearby Carnegie Cultural Center, marking the completion of another round of gatherings before their summer break. Built in 1913, this former Carnegie Library is the perfect spot for their end-of-the-year potluck lunch and the announcement of the upcoming year's book list.

The Book-Enders are mostly adults aged 45 to 80, though anyone is welcome to attend. The group invites special guest speakers to start each meeting, and after a pause for treats and coffee, the members spend the rest of the time discussing the book. Occasionally, the guest speaker also moderates the discussion. When selecting titles, the group only considers one thing: is the book available in paperback? The Friends of the Library generously provide twenty-five copies of each month's book for members to borrow. After the meeting, the gently used copies are sold at a discounted rate.

It is possible that the high quality of guest speakers has helped to contribute to the popularity and longevity of the Book-Enders. For a recent discussion of *All the Light We Cannot See* by Anthony Doerr, Lorene Broersma, an adult services librarian, says the group invited "a French professor who was a former 'Hidden Child,' surviving Nazi-occupied France during World War II with a French foster family." Other meetings have included a Skype visit with author Lisa See after reading *On Gold Mountain* and a talk with a scientist from NASA/JPL for their discussion of *The Martian* by Andy Weir. In the 1990s, when the group read *Fahrenheit 451*, a visit from Ray Bradbury "generated such interest that the meeting had to be changed to a larger venue," Broersma recalls.

# CHAPTER ELEVEN

# PUT IT ONLINE

**N**ot all book clubs need to meet face-to-face. Maybe you have trouble getting patrons to the library because they're too busy or too geographically spread out. Or maybe you have a full slate of in-person book clubs and want to supplement them with a lower-maintenance option for those who can't make it to the library.

Whatever your situation, a digital book club can be a fun and low-intensity way to get your community reading and talking. Here, we'll look at variations on the online book club idea that use different platforms, including Goodreads, Facebook, and themed e-newsletters.

## Leander Readers

**LEANDER PUBLIC LIBRARY | LEANDER, TEXAS**

**COMMUNITY TYPE: SUBURBAN**

https://www.goodreads.com/group/show/509837-leander-readers

Leander Readers is an online book club for adults, hosted on the book-lovers' website Goodreads.com. (The library also offers a YA version, Literally Leander, for teens or adults who like reading YA.)

The Leander Public Library decided to start an online book club in early 2018 to attract new audiences. The library already had an in-person book club, but the attendees were mostly older adults; an online club, they thought, might attract younger people who don't typically come to the library.

They decided on Goodreads, which is a natural forum for hosting online book clubs. Once you're set up with an account, you can add a description of your group, add books to your digital bookshelf, moderate discussions, and promote upcoming events. Members can rate books on a scale of one to five stars, and they can request notifications whenever something is added to one of their threads. Best of all, "most of our members already had a Goodreads account," says Kristen Gerlinger, so the book club fit well into their lifestyles.

Leander Readers reads one staff pick per month, and members post their feedback, at their convenience, in two discussion threads online. The first thread, First Impressions, asks members to share their thoughts about the book before they start reading it, with prompts like "What do you expect to get from this book?" and "How do you feel about this genre?" The second thread, Final Thoughts, invites a conversation about the book's plot, characters, and so on and is meant to be opened after finishing the book. (A note on the book club's Welcome page warns members that Final Thoughts threads contain spoilers.)

A word of advice: Leander Public Library staff learned that members were more likely to post when others had already commented in a thread, so the staff tend to get the ball rolling by commenting first. They've also gotten creative by asking readers to go a step beyond their book club reading. "We've also incorporated some challenges into our forums to get our members to read outside of their comfort zones," says Gerlinger. To be an Alphabet Warrior, readers have a year to read a book whose title starts with each letter of the alphabet; a Genre Mixer reads a book in each of thirty genre categories.

# The Feast

**HUNTSVILLE-MADISON COUNTY PUBLIC LIBRARY | HUNTSVILLE, ALABAMA**

**COMMUNITY TYPE: URBAN**

https://www.facebook.com/groups/TheFeastDowntown

The Feast is a mostly online cookbook club with an in-person smorgasbord. For most of the year, the club exists as a Facebook group where fifty-five members swap recipes for Norwegian meatballs, display photos of their culinary achievements, and share laughs over unappetizing recipes from olden times (tomato and tuna mold, anyone?).

But four times a year, the group gathers in person to sample culinary creations from the library's cookbook collection. To prepare for these potlucks, the library staff transform a large meeting room into a cozy dinner spot: fluorescent lights are swapped for electric candles, tablecloths are laid out, and in the wintertime, a digital fire crackles. Members bring a dish to share and their own plate, silverware, and cup. After introducing themselves and saying a little about their recipe, the participants are free to make casual conversation—"just like you would at a real dinner party," says the book club's leader, Suzanne Flynn.

Each dinner has a theme. One recent potluck asked each member to bring a dish from a different country, ensuring a diverse menu and good representation from the library's international cookbook collection. Another theme challenged members to cook any recipe by the best-selling cookbook author Christy Jordan, who focuses on Southern cuisine.

The potlucks also serve as promotion for library-goers who might not have heard of the club. During the international feast, a patron wandered into the room wondering what was going on. "Once she found out that it was international food night, she turned around and ran out, driving home and grabbing some food so she could return and partake," Flynn says. "She arrived out of breath with some delicious roasted artichokes."

One word of warning: be sure to consider food allergies. Flynn includes a statement that the dishes may contain allergens or may have been cooked in a kitchen with allergens.

# Y(A) Not? An Online Book Club for Adults Who Read YA

**SHARON PUBLIC LIBRARY | SHARON, MASSACHUSETTS**
**COMMUNITY TYPE: SUBURBAN**
https://conta.cc/2LwZAOb

Online book clubs can allow for differing levels of interaction between members, depending on the platform they utilize. On the low-interaction end of the spectrum is Y(A) Not?, a newsletter-based book club for adult lovers of young adult fiction.

"There is a significant section of the adult reading population who enjoy reading YA literature for different reasons," says book club leader Hilary Umbreit. Some are actually emerging adults, who are YA books' target demographic—but there are also parents who are interested in what their teenagers are reading, or adults who just enjoy the stories, themes, or style of YA literature. "We settled on a digital format because we felt it would appeal to a wider span of potential readers, and especially emerging adults who spend a lot of time on social media and might prefer an asynchronous option to a more traditional meeting structure."

Distributed monthly to people who have signed up for the Y(A) Not list, the newsletter includes book recommendations (with links to the books' Goodreads pages), related articles, and author information. Each newsletter is themed: "Head Out on the Highway: Road Trips, Quests & Journeys," for example, plugged summery stories about cross-country drives, memorable getaways, and personal voyages of self-discovery. January featured "The Best YA Books of 2017," and June's "Out Loud and Proud" issue commemorated Pride Month with fiction by LGBTQIA+ authors or featuring queer protagonists.

While it has no required reading and no discussion to facilitate, Y(A) Not still requires staff time to research and build each issue in the e-marketing platform Constant Contact. "Our primary concern in selecting which titles to include is to make sure that the books represent a diverse array of authentic experiences and voices," Umbreit says. "The #OwnVoices movement, for example, has been indispensable in reviewing titles."

## Online Book Club

**BERKELEY COLLEGE LIBRARY | PARAMUS, NEW JERSEY**

COMMUNITY TYPE: URBAN

https://berkeleycollege.libguides.com/onlinebookclub

Berkeley College has seven physical campuses throughout New York and New Jersey, plus more than 1,200 online students across the United States and abroad. The college's library needed a book club that could engage the whole community. The result: the Online Book Club, which invites students, faculty, and staff to read a new title each semester, discuss the book online, and attend a talk by the author, either on campus or online.

Students have three weeks to respond to discussion questions on Goodreads; the library recruits student leaders who help facilitate the discussions. The author events are held at one of Berkeley College's campuses and are livestreamed. The talks consist of a 30-minute presentation and a 45-minute Q&A, during which online students can ask questions by chat. Students at the live event have the chance to get their books signed and take a photo with the author.

Past speakers have included Kevin Kruse (*15 Secrets Successful People Know about Time Management*) and Sampson Davis (*Living and Dying in Brick City: An ER Doctor Returns Home*). Some author events get more than 300 students tuning in live.

The key to this solid turnout? "Our book club thrives on faculty support," says Matthew LaBrake, senior director of online library and technology services. "Since we are a career college, books that teach students important life and academic skills are well received. The faculty often offer students extra credit for participating in our online discussions, and bring their classes to the live author event, or screen the event in their classes at different campuses."

Another perk: the library gives away a limited number of free copies of the books—for keeps. Students who snag a free book must commit to participating in the Goodreads discussion.

# CHAPTER TWELVE

# GET THEM MEETING AT AN EARLY AGE

**I**f you think you struggle with consistent attendance for your adult book club, you should know that this is even more of an issue when creating a book club for kids or teens. Reading an assigned book every month for a meeting can often feel like more homework, and other after-school commitments can make it difficult to find the time to read.

Libraries are actively combating this notion in creative ways. Inviting parents or teachers to join the club, partnering with other organizations, reading the book at the meeting, and allowing members to have free choice over what they read are all ways to increase participation in book clubs for youth.

## Family Book Club

**BOSTON PUBLIC LIBRARY, ADAMS STREET BRANCH**
**DORCHESTER, MASSACHUSETTS**
COMMUNITY TYPE: URBAN

Partnering with the Leahy Holloran Community Center led to the creation of the Family Book Club. Meaghan Schwelm, a children's librarian at the Boston Public Library, says, "Through this unique partnership, we have been able to tap into the community center's resources as well as the library's resources."

The book club members are children in grades 3–6, who attend with an adult family member. The meeting location alternates between the library and the community center and begins with a family-style dinner of pizza and salad. Because of the participants' age range, selecting books that are both appealing and age-appropriate for all can be challenging. "If someone has a suggestion and it's not quite right for your group, make an effort to find something similar," advises Schwelm.

The Family Book Club actually began meeting before Schwelm started working at the library, but she has since taken over the club and added her own flair. In addition to the book discussion, the meetings now include an activity related to the book. After reading *Roller Girl* by Victoria Jamieson, Schwelm invited skaters from local Roller Derby leagues to join the discussion. She also provided rental skates to all the children in attendance so they could practice their moves alongside their special guests. During another meeting, Jerel Dye, a local illustrator, led a cartooning workshop for the group.

Members of the group have also contributed to designing the special activities for their meetings. After reading *Book Scavenger* by Jennifer Chambliss Bertmen, one child developed a complicated book scavenger hunt that involved ciphers and riddles throughout the library. Schwelm notes, "Jane received a round of applause for her cleverly crafted challenge."

To host a successful book club, Schwelm advises libraries to look for a local partner that can contribute either financially or with other resources. She also thinks that the staff's enthusiasm for the program is crucial. "Sharing food, casual conversation, and a love of reading has kept members engaged and coming back," says Schwelm.

## Harry Potter Reading Club

**CABOT PUBLIC LIBRARY | CABOT, ARKANSAS**
COMMUNITY TYPE: SUBURBAN

Like many people around the world, Kirsten Seidel, the YA/adult services librarian at the Cabot Public Library, loves Harry Potter. The Harry Potter Reading Club was born from her enthusiasm for The Boy Who Lived. Seidel says, "I think that when we as librarians provide programming about books and topics we're passionate about, our patrons are aware of it, get excited about it because we're excited about it, and they want to be a part of that program."

Meeting since September 2016, the Harry Potter Reading Club is largely made up of preteens (ages eight to fourteen) and their families. They read each Harry Potter book in sections, getting together twice a month to discuss the selected chapters for that meeting and participate in related activities. Over the years, Seidel notes, "our discussions have evolved from a simple Q&A (which started to get pretty stale) to different activities that engage the whole group (even the parents!)."

The Internet, and Pinterest specifically, have inspired many of the activities Seidel has used with this group. Harry Potter–themed crafts are always a hit. Members have made Sorcerer's Stones, pine cone Hedwigs, mini mandrakes, and wands. Games like Harry Potter Would You Rather, Harry Potter Jeopardy, Harry Potter Bingo, and Harry Potter Pyramid have also been well received. Seidel has even managed to incorporate math with a Gringotts activity.

Other meetings have included more complicated and large-scale activities, to the delight of both the children and their parents. When the group read *Harry Potter and the Sorcerer's Stone*, families participated in a sorting ceremony at the library. Wizard duels and Quidditch games, activities that would certainly not be tolerated by Madam Pince in the Hogwarts Library, have also occurred. They even held a Honeydukes sweets tasting during one of their *Harry Potter and the Prisoner of Azkaban* discussions.

The Harry Potter Reading Club is proof that personal connections can be an asset to library programming. "Don't be scared to let your inner geek out to influence your book clubs. I think a big reason why this club was successful was both because it is a popular series, and because it's a series that is near and dear to my heart," says Seidel.

# Starbooks Book Club

**VERNON HILLS HIGH SCHOOL LIBRARY MEDIA CENTER**

**VERNON HILLS, ILLINOIS**

COMMUNITY TYPE: SUBURBAN

For the last twelve years, students have gathered at the Vernon Hills High School Library Media Center for book club meetings. Although it started out as a more traditional book club, with everyone reading the same book each month, school librarian Monica Tolva revamped the format and named it the Starbooks Book Club to combat dwindling participation. "We patterned our book club after that great coffee place [Starbucks] down the street," she says. Adopting a more relaxed atmosphere and emphasizing a common love of books helped students see the club as a welcoming place to meet every Friday before school.

To combat the homework vibes that come along with required reading, the members are now free to read books of their choice. They are encouraged to try some of the books nominated for the Illinois Teen Choice Award, but with twenty titles to choose from, there are a variety of options to appeal to everyone. Tolva keeps a list of all titles discussed in each meeting that members can access on their website. During one memorable meeting, the group held a white elephant book swap, with each member contributing a wrapped book. In describing the event, Tolva says, "Much screaming (fourteen-year-old girls do that, you know!) and fun. Many promises to share and swap again later."

Additionally, the members also participate in other school and community activities. Three times a year, they are responsible for running the school's concessions stand and are able to use the profits for book club supplies. The group has completed several volunteer projects, including collecting donations of children's books. They also attempt to brighten the day of their fellow students. "We make bookmarks or sticky notes with reading encouragement and hide them in the library's collection," says Tolva.

Rather than just advertise the Starbooks Book Club with flyers, Tolva has developed a creative way of involving her members in the marketing process. "We print the club's coffeehouse-themed logo on cup sleeves and stickers, and the students leave carrying their cups for all to see," she says. In addition to warming them up every Friday morning, their hot chocolate serves as a way for members to share their love of books and reading with the entire student body.

## Banned Book Club

**PARIS MIDDLE SCHOOL LIBRARY | PARIS, ARKANSAS**
**COMMUNITY TYPE: RURAL**

Most libraries host events or put up displays during Banned Book Week, but Anne Canada, the library media specialist at the Paris Middle School Library, wanted to continue these conversations throughout the school year. As a result, eighth-graders and their parents have been participating in the Banned Book Club at the library since 2010. "My pitch to parents is that the world is not censored and that books offer us a platform to discuss tough issues," says Canada.

The Banned Book Club begins meeting every year during Banned Book Week. While Canada talks to all of the students about the First Amendment, she also discusses the importance of developing informed opinions with the eighth-graders. The school library hosts several free book clubs, but Canada does charge a fee for the Banned Book Club in order to make sure that parents are aware of the group. The funds are used to purchase T-shirts and copies of each month's book for every member.

Popular titles have included *Speak* by Laurie Halse Anderson, *The Absolutely True Diary of a Part-Time Indian* by Sherman Alexie, and *Looking for Alaska* by John Green. Reading *Staying Fat for Sarah Byrnes* by Chris Crutcher was particularly memorable because they invited the author to visit the school. During his visit, he had lunch with members of the book club. Describing the conversation, Canada says, "I was impressed at the maturity and daring of the questions."

In the United States, books are generally banned because the topics within their pages are controversial in some way. While reading banned books provides a chance for members of the book club to engage in meaningful discussions, it can also make some students feel uncomfortable sharing their opinions. Canada has found an interesting solution to this problem. She notes, "I've done online discussions of books in real time where kids get to choose a name for the duration of the book club, and what's cool is that the room is silent, but the discussion becomes *loud* as kids type fast and furious."

# SPUB Club (Super Popular, Unbelievable Book Club)

**MILTON PUBLIC LIBRARY | MILTON, MASSACHUSETTS**

**COMMUNITY TYPE: SUBURBAN**

Sara Truog, the assistant director of the Milton Public Library, wanted to provide her younger patrons with a chance to discuss books, but she was struggling to find an appealing format. She says: "Traditional book clubs for kids tend not to work at my library because there's an element of homework to having to read a book in advance of the meeting." Instead, she decided to try her luck with a read-aloud club. The members participate in activities that encourage active listening while Truog reads a chapter book to them. Popular activities have included Play-Doh, Legos, Wikki Stix, drawing, Rubik's Cubes, Geoboards, scratch art, and other crafts.

Members of the SPUB Club particularly enjoy reading humorous stories. *Choose Your Own Adventure* books, *The Adventures of Nanny Piggins* by R. A. Spratt, and *Alvin Ho: Allergic to Girls, School, and Other Scary Things* by Lenore Look have all been hits with the group. While reading *The Adventures of Nanny Piggins*, members thought it was hilarious when a character shouted, "Great balls of fire!" Truog told the club she would give a prize to anyone who could say this to her outside of the book club. She recalls, "The following week I ran into one of the students at a school event and she shouted, 'Great balls of fire!' at me right in the middle of the high school auditorium! Needless to say, she won the prize."

Truog acknowledges that it can be challenging to sustain the membership of a kids' book club. After two years together, she thinks one of the main draws of the SPUB Club is that members don't have to read anything before attending the meetings. She also recommends attracting additional members by holding a "Bring a Friend" evening at the start of a new book.

## Lakeside Book Club

**LAKESIDE JUNIOR HIGH SCHOOL | SPRINGDALE, ARKANSAS**

COMMUNITY TYPE: SUBURBAN AND RURAL

Brian Johnson, the library/media specialist at Lakeside Junior High School's Dr. Don Love Library, started the Lakeside Book Club, also known as LBC, after repeatedly hearing his students say, "Mr. J, I have no books at home." Determined to both provide his students with books and develop their love of reading, he regularly applies for grants to ensure that he can purchase copies of every book for each member of the LBC.

Each cycle of the LBC runs for six to eight weeks, with the members discussing one book for the entire cycle. While Johnson hopes to reach reluctant readers, the book club is open to all eighth- and ninth-grade students, as well as teachers. Popular titles have included *Bright Lights, Dark Nights* by Stephen Emond, *Orbiting Jupiter* by Gary Schmidt, and *Wolf by Wolf* by Ryan Graudin. Each cycle begins with a guest speaker. Past guests have included an anthropology professor from Canada, the school's resource officer, and Dr. Don Love himself. The book club also connects with the author of the book over Skype, e-mail, or social media.

Conversations about the books don't just take place within the walls of the library. "It is not uncommon to have a student member mention that they have started communicating on a higher level with their parent/family through discussing the books we read," Johnson notes. He says many of the students share their new books with both their family and friends, spreading their passion for reading throughout their community.

Johnson utilizes the school-wide broadcast to promote the book club, and he features advertisements on the library's digital screens. On one memorable occasion, he let members know that he would be announcing the next cycle's book selection on the screens. He recalls, "It ended up being *Wolf by Wolf,* and the students became silent when they saw the announcement was about to post. They were literally jumping up and down with excitement and screaming because they were so excited to read that work!"

## Get Outside Book Club

**DAYTON METRO LIBRARY | DAYTON, OHIO**
COMMUNITY TYPE: SUBURBAN

In 2009, the Dayton Metro Library and the Five Rivers MetroParks, a regional park system that protects over 16,000 acres, shared a common desire for members in their community. A partnership between the two organizations led to the formation of the Get Outside Book Club. Dorri Hegyi, a children's services librarian, says, "The main idea was that parents and children spend time together reading and experiencing nature, building pre-literacy skills and positive attitudes toward nature."

From September 1 to October 31 every year, families with preschoolers and day-care kids are invited to read six nature-themed books and participate in related outdoor activities. While families are encouraged to select their own books, there are resources available for anyone in need of suggestions. A few books that proved popular with the participating families have included *Mud Fairy* by Amy Young, *Cloudette* by Tom Lichtenheld, and *Leaf Man* by Lois Ehlert.

While the book club is in session, the Dayton Metro Library holds nature-themed storytimes both at its branches and at the Five Rivers MetroParks. The library and the parks work together to promote the book club in their community on social media, in local parenting publications, and on the local television channels. One challenge that regularly presents itself is the weather—but for Hegyi, even rain cannot put a damper on some experiences. As she says, "Children handling a spider bigger than their own hand is always memorable."

While partnering with the Five Rivers MetroParks has certainly contributed to the book club's success, Hegyi thinks it would be fairly easy for other libraries to replicate this group, even without the support of local parks. Ultimately, she says, "children are naturally curious about their world. They want to know what things are, how they work, and what they can do." Libraries are the perfect place for families to explore these concepts by utilizing the collection and extending their children's new knowledge into an outdoor activity.

# CONCLUSION

**As we were** writing this book, we were continuously amazed by the creativity and dedication of book club leaders across the country. While we couldn't feature every club in these pages, we were impressed with each book club we came across in our research. We hope you have found these book clubs to be inspirational as you begin your journey to start a new group or refresh an old group.

While the collection of book clubs you've just read about varies wildly, many of their leaders have one thing in common: they weren't always immediately successful. Sure, some of these leaders found the million-dollar idea right away, but most people had to try at least one or two iterations before they found the right book club for their community.

The biggest lesson you should take away from this book is that every community is different, and not every book club format will work in every community. Don't be afraid to fail. Every time you do, you'll learn something that can be applied to a future book club.

You won't always get it right on the first try, but don't let that stop you from reinventing the book club and trying again until you find the perfect fit.

# RESOURCES

## BOOK SELECTION AND DISCUSSION RESOURCES

### LitLovers

www.litlovers.com
LitLovers provides a wide variety of discussion guides, book reviews, and general information on starting a book club. Their LitFood guide is perfect for groups wishing to incorporate food into their book club.

### Goodreads

https://www.goodreads.com
Goodreads is a website devoted to readers' advisory service. Not only can members of the site share books among themselves, but they can also discover books through recommendations that Goodreads makes based on a member's past favorites.

### Book Browse

https://www.bookbrowse.com/bookclubs
BookBrowse provides reading group guides, book reviews, advice, online discussions, and other great material in the Book Clubs section of their website. They also put out an e-newsletter that highlights these topics.

## PUBLISHERS' BOOK CLUB RESOURCES

### Random House Reader's Circle

www.randomhousebooks.com/brand/random-house-readers-circle
Random House Reader's Circle is an e-newsletter that provides book recommendations, author interviews, giveaways, and other useful materials for book clubs.

## Reading Group Center

http://knopfdoubleday.com/reading-group-center
Reading Group Center, a website of Knopf Doubleday, includes an e-newsletter, reading group guides and tips, and book recommendations. Book clubs can also schedule author chats for their meetings on this site.

## Read It Forward

https://www.readitforward.com
Penguin Random House's Read It Forward website provides visitors with book recommendations, articles, author interviews and essays, and giveaways. In addition to content on the website, Read It Forward also produces a podcast and an e-newsletter.

## Book Club Favorites

www.simonandschuster.com/bookclubs
Every month, Simon and Schuster's Book Club Favorites website provides resources for book clubs to discuss a particular title. The site offers book club kits that can be downloaded, and a chance for an entire club to win copies of the book. For people who are not currently in a book club, there is a Facebook group where an online book discussion takes place throughout the month.

## Sourcebooks: For Book Clubs & Reading Groups

https://www.sourcebooks.com/bookclubs.html
This website provides discussion guides, an e-newsletter, and book recommendations. It also features a food and beverage guide that can be used to find tasty treats for your meetings.

## HC Book Club

https://www.harpercollins.com/bookclub
The HC Book Club, presented by HarperCollins and Book Club Girl, suggests multiple book titles every month for book clubs. Each suggestion comes with a variety of resources, including discussion guides, author videos, and podcasts. The site also sends out an e-newsletter.

### Reading Group Gold

https://us.macmillan.com/reading-group-gold
MacMillan's Reading Group Gold website provides discussion guides, book recommendations, related recipes for book club meetings, and an e-newsletter.
Visitors to the site can also request advance reading copies of upcoming books
and invite an author to attend a book club meeting.

## CELEBRITY BOOK CLUBS

### Our Shared Shelf

https://www.goodreads.com/group/show/179584-our-shared-shelf
The English actress Emma Watson began the feminist book club Our Shared Shelf
in January 2016. New titles are selected every two months, and participants are
invited to post their thoughts on the group's Goodreads page.

### Reese's Book Club x Hello Sunshine

https://hello-sunshine.com/book-club
The actress Reese Witherspoon founded Reese's Book Club x Hello Sunshine in
June 2017. Information about the current book, previous titles, and relevant
articles can be found on this website.

### Oprah's Book Club

www.oprah.com/app/books.html
In 1996, Oprah Winfrey began Oprah's Book Club as part of the *Oprah Winfrey
Show*. Although the show stopped airing in 2011, Oprah's Book Club continues
online. This site provides book recommendations, articles, author interviews, an
e-newsletter, and information about each month's book selection.

## NATIONAL BOOK CLUB INITIATIVES

### Book Club Central

www.bookclubcentral.org
Book Club Central was developed in 2017 as an initiative of the American Library
Association. The actress Sarah Jessica Parker is the honorary chair and announced

her first book selection at the ALA Annual Conference in June 2017 in Chicago. Visitors to the site will find current and past SJP Picks for the club, as well as an abundance of advice on starting and maintaining a book club, book recommendations, and much more.

## Great Stories Club

www.ala.org/greatstories

The American Library Association's Great Stories Club is a reading and discussion program that gives underserved youth the opportunity to read, reflect, and share ideas on topics that resonate with them. Library workers can apply to receive a Great Stories Club grant; recipients receive training, copies of books to gift to their book club members, and other resources to help them lead book clubs with small groups of teens. Since the program was created in 2006, more than 700 libraries in 49 states have used this model with over 30,000 teens and young adults, ages thirteen to twenty-one. The programs' resources (humanities content, discussion questions, etc.) are available to all, free of charge, on the website.

## National Reading Group Month

www.nationalreadinggroupmonth.com

National Reading Group Month was created by the Women's National Book Association. During the month of October, people are encouraged to join a book group or start a new club, and existing book clubs are encouraged to celebrate their success. A calendar of events and book suggestions are just a few of the things that can be found on this site.

## ilovelibraries

www.ilovelibraries.org/booklovers/bookclub

The Starting a Book Club section on ilovelibraries provides questions to consider when getting started, tips for meetings and discussions, book ideas, and a list of other helpful resources.

## BOOK CLUBS TO FOLLOW

### Barnes and Noble Book Club

https://www.barnesandnoble.com/h/book-club
Each season, people will gather at Barnes & Noble bookstores across the country
on the same day to discuss one book. This website provides information about
the current selection, interviews with the author, and links to the B&N Podcast.

### Chicago Booksellers Book Club

https://twitter.com/chibooksellers?lang=en
The Chicago Booksellers Book Club first met in April 2018. Developed as a way
for booksellers in Chicago to get together and talk about upcoming books, the
group gathers every two months.

## BOOKS AND ARTICLES ABOUT BOOK CLUBS

### *The Librarian's Guide to Book Programs and Author Events*, by Brad Hooper

https://www.alastore.ala.org/content/librarians-guide-book-programs
-and-author-events
This how-to guide shares practical steps for hosting book clubs and other book-re-
lated programming.

### *After-School Clubs for Kids: Thematic Programming to Encourage Reading*, by Lisa M. Shaia

https://www.alastore.ala.org/content/after-school-clubs-kids-thematic
-programming-encourage-reading
If you were inspired by our chapter on book clubs for kids, check out this book
for even more fun ideas.

### "The State of the Book Club," by Casey Blue James, November 2016

http://authornews.penguinrandomhouse.com/the-state-of-the-book-club/
Addressing how book clubs have changed over the years, this article includes
book club statistics and tips for authors looking to connect with book clubs.

# INDEX